Typographica

Typographica   Rick Poynor

Princeton Architectural Press   New York

Published by
Princeton Architectural Press
37 East 7th Street
New York, New York 10003

For a free catalog of books, call 1.800.722.6657
Visit our web site at www.papress.com

Simultaneously published in London by
Laurence King Publishing
an imprint of Calmann & King Ltd

Printed and bound in Hong Kong
05 04 03 02 5 4 3 2 1 First edition

Designed by Stephen Coates, August, London
Photography by Nigel Jackson

Library of Congress Cataloging-in-Publication
Data for this title is available from the
Publisher

ISBN: 1-56898-298-4

Contents

Preface

I first met Herbert Spencer by chance in the early 1990s, when we found ourselves sitting next to each other waiting for a lecture to begin at London's Design Museum. I was then editor of *Eye* magazine, just a few issues old at the time, and delighted to discover that he was a subscriber. His enthusiasm was especially pleasing because his own magazine, *Typographica*, was one of the main inspirations for starting *Eye*. I sometimes consulted *Typographica* as a historical document, a source of useful information, but its appeal was much broader. It lay in the way that Spencer, as designer, editor and sometimes writer, was able to integrate these usually separate tasks in a long-running publishing experiment that went well beyond the norms and conventions of a typical design journal. I learned a great deal, as an editor, from studying how Spencer achieved these rich editorial and visual effects.

As a magazine, *Typographica* was obviously not a one-man show. It relied on the collaboration of many individuals prepared to contribute to its pages without much reward. Nevertheless, it was a much less 'collective' endeavour than a publication such as its contemporary, *Design*, also launched in 1949. *Design*'s official purpose was to express the promotional aims and policies of a national organization, the Council of Industrial Design; *Typographica* came into being because an individual – Spencer – wanted it to exist and was lucky enough to encounter a publisher prepared to underwrite his youthful project, while leaving it entirely in his hands. *Design*, during the 18 years of *Typographica*'s

existence, had four editors, five art editors and a changing cast of supporting personnel; *Typographica* was edited and designed, from the first issue to the last, by Spencer alone. *Design* was produced, like most professionally-run magazines, in its publisher's offices; *Typographica* was created in its editor's studio, where he enjoyed a degree of autonomy in deciding its content, direction, physical composition and long-term evolution that was comparatively rare in periodical publishing at the time, and is even rarer today.

A year or so after that first meeting, I began to consider the possibility of studying *Typographica* in depth. A preliminary survey revealed that, other than contemporary reviews and a few journalists' profiles, nothing substantial had been written about the magazine. Nor, it seemed, had it ever been the subject of postgraduate research. This was the path I decided to take. As an area of study, graphic design history is still in its infancy and, so far, little attention has been paid to the formative years of the profession. There is, as yet, no single historical study tracing the development of commercial art and graphic design practice in Britain in the twentieth century, and no unified account of the professionalization of graphic design in the post-war years and of the forces that gave it shape. By examining the nature, role, impact and implications of this highly ambitious publication, I hoped to contribute to a more detailed understanding not only of *Typographica*, but of the period of graphic design history in which, it seemed to me, it had played a crucial part. In 1993,

I began my MPhil research at the Royal College of Art under the supervision of Dr Alex Seago, whose book about *Ark* magazine – another of *Typographica*'s contemporaries – gave further impetus to my own inquiries when it was published in 1995.

This project could never have been undertaken without the cooperation of Herbert Spencer and I owe him a great debt of thanks. For seven years he has tolerated my never-ending questions – in formal interviews and casual conversations – with inexhaustible patience, generosity and good humour. He allowed me open access to his home, his memories of working on the magazine, and his archives. My thanks, too, to Marianne Spencer for her hospitality and for giving me an interview. The following *Typographica* colleagues and contributors also agreed to be interviewed about those years: Alan Fletcher, Ken Garland, John Commander, Colin Forbes, John Taylor, Jasia Reichardt, Brian Little, Alan Bartram, Derek Birdsall, Richard Hollis, Richard Hamilton, Hansje Oorthuys, Michael Middleton, James Sutton, Philip Thompson, Robin Fior and Romek Marber. Many thanks to all of you for giving me your time.

My main supervisor at the RCA, Dr Jeremy Aynsley, was a constant source of insight and encouragement; our meetings were always a pleasure. My thanks to Jeremy, to Professor Christopher Frayling and to Dr Penny Sparke for their support. Jeremy asked me to present early findings at the Association of Art Historians' 21st Annual Conference at the Victoria & Albert Museum in April 1995, and Steven Heller gave me a similar opportunity in New York, at the eighth 'Modernism & Eclecticism' conference, in February 1995. Conversations with Robin Kinross have also been enormously helpful in focusing my thoughts; thanks, too, for the information supplied. Pauline Rae and the librarians of the Royal College of Art made a vital contribution. Thanks to Dr David Mellor for agreeing to examine this research in its earlier thesis form, to Laurence King, Jo Lightfoot and Kevin Lippert for seeing its potential as a book, and to Stephen Coates at August for his excellent design.

Most of the visual material illustrated in these pages is drawn from Herbert Spencer's personal archive or my own collection. For supplying images or for permission to use them, I thank: Jasia Reichardt and Nick Wadley at the Themerson Archive, Robert Harling, Roger Mayne, Robert Freeman, Ken Garland, John Berger and Jean Mohr, Ian Hamilton Finlay, Peter Blake, Richard Hamilton, Jackie Monnier, Ivan Chermayeff, Tom Geismar, Alan Fletcher, Colin Forbes, Hulton Getty, and the Royal College of Art. Every effort has been made to contact copyright holders, where known, and any oversights will be rectified in future editions. Please contact the publisher.

Last – and above all – I must thank Jane and Rachel for enduring the loss of so many weekends and having the kindness not to protest.

Rick Poynor

TYPOGRAPHICA 1

1.

New formations

Typographica is one of the most distinctive visual arts publications of the post-war period. It was published in London, in two series of 16 issues each, from 1949 to 1967, when its editor, Herbert Spencer, and publisher/printer, Lund Humphries, took the decision to bring the magazine to a halt. By any standards it was a considerable achievement and one with few close parallels in the art and design publishing of its time. *Typographica* is unusual not just for the consistency of its editorial vision but for its longevity, since this was a magazine that made and – more surprisingly – was expected to make no profit for its gentlemanly owners. Only 25 when he started *Typographica*, Spencer edited it, designed it, wrote many of the articles and kept it going for 18 years, while pursuing a career as typographer, design consultant, author, editor and teacher that would establish him, at a precociously early age, as one of the more notable figures in British typography and graphic design. ≫→

Typographica, 0S no. 1, 1949. Design: Spencer

Typographica was never as typographically focused or as narrowly professional in its concerns as its choice of name might suggest. Spencer introduced British and international readers to path-finding modernists such as Kurt Schwitters, Alexander Rodchenko, El Lissitzky, Piet Zwart, Paul Schuitema, Herbert Bayer, Henryk Berlewi and Max Bill, but he also retained an interest in such traditional subjects as early horse racing programmes, tombstone lettering, printers' stock blocks and the Royal Arms. From the outset, he included articles on abstract painting and book illustration. As the magazine developed, and Spencer grew in confidence, he began to expose his printer and designer readers to avant-garde material that fell well outside the usual remit and range of a 'typography' publication: Stefan and Franciszka Themerson's Gaberbocchus Press; the word art of Josua Reichert; the abstract drawings of Alcopley; concrete poets Diter Rot and Ian Hamilton Finlay; Richard Hamilton's typographic reconstruction of Marcel Duchamp's *Green Box*.

In the more elaborate second series (1960–67), photography became increasingly central to *Typographica*, not only as a subject, but as a visual tool that allowed a new way of conceiving and 'writing' the magazine. This, too, was a modernist idea, as *Typographica* implicitly acknowledged in 1964, when contributor Michael Middleton quoted László Moholy-Nagy: 'The knowledge of photography is just as important as that of the alphabet. The illiterate of the future will be the person ignorant of the use of the camera as well as of the pen.'[1] *Typographica* was modernist in a much broader and richer sense than the few typographically-minded commentators who have written about it in passing, over the years, tend to allow.[2]

Encountered for the first time, the issues of the second series are highly seductive. The thick paper wrap-around covers have an instant, cool-to-the-touch appeal, a substantial and satisfying heaviness. The colour is vibrant and there is a simplicity and clarity to the pages that still looks contemporary and fresh. Coated and uncoated papers, thick sugar papers and delicate overlays are mixed together, sometimes in a single issue. Elaborate use is made of throw-outs, gatefolds, special bound-in insets, and booklets attached to the body of the publication by a thread. *Typographica*'s compelling physical form, its visual and tactile rhetoric, was a persuasive part of its argument for a new graphic and typographic design. It was a designed object to a degree that few design periodicals achieve, particularly over such an extended period. Issues still feature regularly in the catalogues of specialist booksellers and designers continue to track down copies and collect it.

Many of those who reviewed *Typographica* in its day were perplexed by the magazine's more esoteric subjects, even as they admired the excellence of its presswork and the usefulness of its practical features. Articles that strayed too far from the norms and values of the typographic scene were likely to be greeted in tones of parental reproof. Design commentary from

10

Herbert Spencer, 1954

within the profession has frequently acted to establish and monitor acceptable limits for practice.[3] Those appraisals that come closest to understanding what *Typographica* was about – as, for instance, a review by Germano Facetti in 1961 – are invariably brief and undeveloped. 'The magazine now bridges the gap between practice, theory and history that most instruments of communication for designers seem unable, unwilling or impotent to do,' Facetti concludes his sympathetic notice.[4] This tantalizing judgement, from a key figure in British graphic design of the 1960s, accurately summarizes the challenge to conventional disciplinary boundaries made by Spencer's ground-breaking journal.

What is so interesting about *Typographica* in retrospect is that it constantly implies through visual and textual juxtaposition, as well as its highly personal and idiosyncratic mixture of subject matter, a fusion of commercial printing and aesthetic experiment that it can never fully articulate or resolve in its writing and commentary. These tensions are frequently manifest in the remarks made in the magazine and elsewhere by Spencer and his contributors. Beyond *Typographica*'s immediate impact and influence on close contemporaries, in the 1950s and early 1960s, Spencer's preoccupations would eventually come to make a contribution that he could not have foreseen and, if he had, might well have opposed.[5]

Since the 1980s, a fusion of commerce and the typographic avant-garde has come about, partly as a result of new digital technology, which gave designers an unprecedented degree of typographic freedom. Spencer may have been constrained as a typographer by the 'prevailing views and institutional structures' of his time, as Robin Kinross suggests in *Modern Typography*, but his tastes, instincts and practice as an editor-designer – if not always his commentary and arguments – both anticipated and helped to facilitate these developments.[6] As Dick Higgins, American experimental artist and publisher, has observed, *Typographica*, 'was not only extraordinarily elegant and handsome, but was also avant-garde in the best sense of the term, a sort of harbinger of larger-scale interest to come'.[7]

Spencer's *Pioneers of Modern Typography*, first published in 1969, two years after *Typographica*'s demise, is a book very much in the magazine's spirit. It brings together short illustrated profiles of many of the modernist artists and designers previously published in its pages by Spencer.[8] In the late 1970s, at the start of the postmodern period in British graphic design, *Pioneers* was filleted for ideas by young revivalist designers such as Malcolm Garrett, Peter Saville and Neville Brody, and a few years later by Why Not Associates.[9] The typographic experiments of the 1920s modernists, first seen by many British designers in *Typographica*, offered a liberating alternative model to the continuing dominance of the 'idea' graphics invented in New York in the late 1950s.

A reappraisal of Spencer's contribution as editor, designer and catalyst is not only timely, but essential to help establish a context for the far-reaching changes to typographic communication in the 1980s and 1990s, particularly as they apply to British graphic design. The new 'new typography' of the digital era rejected the overt assumptions and teaching of Spencer and his like-minded post-war contemporaries, while seizing the possibilities for cross-fertilization and the transgression of disciplinary boundaries that Spencer's practice as editor of *Typographica* and author of *Pioneers of Modern Typography* had implied and prefigured but been unable to make explicit.[10] As some writers have argued, such possibilities can only be understood by taking a much less prescriptive view of typographic practice than has been typical of existing commentaries and histories. These tend to come from inside the design profession and serve to endorse and legitimize professional assumptions rather than to interrogate or expand them.[11]

To establish the full significance of a publication that Spencer himself singles out as one of his most durable achievements, it is therefore necessary at times to read against the stated intentions and conscious interpretations of its editor. Spencer's editorial obsessions and intuitively determined juxtapositions gave rise to possibilities and suggested meanings that he himself did not necessarily intend or predict. *Typographica*'s innovation was to presuppose, through these collisions – rather than through any elaborate theoretical statement – threads of aesthetic, intellectual and sometimes practical connection between its spectacularly disparate parts.

Spencer's inquiring openness and non-prescriptive modernism are the very qualities that make his editorial eclecticism possible.[12] Like its contemporary, *Ark*, the Royal College of Art magazine edited and designed by the London college's students, *Typographica*'s celebration of cultural pluralism anticipates the emergence of a fully postmodern sensibility in British art and design; and, as with *Ark*, this is far from a fully conscious programme. 'As a reflection of this cultural "moment",' writes Alex Seago, '*Ark* was most successful when it was intuitive rather than intellectual, semi-coherent rather than didactic.'[13] In much the same way, but with even greater aesthetic invention, *Typographica*'s suggestiveness lies in its totality, as an exceptionally prescient amalgam of writing, editing and design.

11

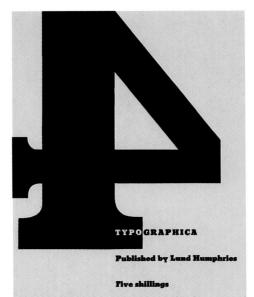

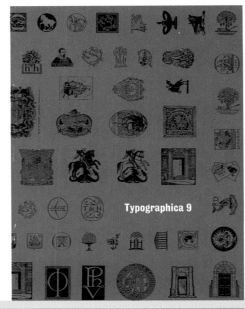

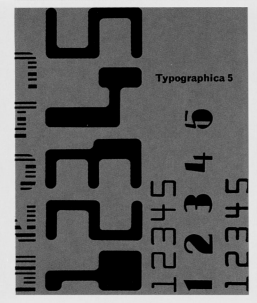

Typographica covers
Top: OS no. 4, 1951. Design: Spencer.
Top centre: OS no. 7, 1953. Design: Edward Wright.
Top right: OS no. 9, 1954. Design: Spencer, using publishers' colophons.

Above: NS no. 5, June 1962. Design: Spencer, using characters for automatic reading.
Right: NS no. 6, December 1962. Design: Spencer, using braille.

14

Typographica 7

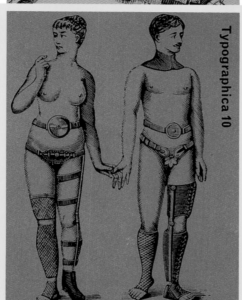

Typographica 10

Above left: OS no. 12, 1956.
Design: Spencer, using
revived nineteenth-century
characters.
Above centre: OS no. 13,
1957. Design: Spencer, using
French book club designs
and drawings by Avigdor
Arikha.
Above: OS no. 14, 1958.
Design: Spencer.

Far left: NS no. 7, May 1963.
Design: Spencer, using
details of typography
featured in 'Typography in
Britain today' exhibition.
Left: NS no. 10, December
1964. Design: Spencer.
Below left: NS no. 14,
December 1966. Design:
Crosby/Fletcher/Forbes.
Below: NS no. 15, June 1967.
Design: Crosby/
Fletcher/Forbes.

13

Herbert Spencer was born in Clapton, London on 22 June 1924, to Harold and Ellen Spencer. His father was a water systems engineer, based in Bloomsbury; he has a younger sister, Joan. There was no family interest in the arts, or connection with that world. 'I became passionately interested in printing at the age of 12,' Spencer recalls. 'I don't remember what sparked it off, or why printing had this extraordinary fascination for me.'[14] The discovery that types came in different sizes and designs came as a 'tremendous shock'.[15] His curiosity led him to visit small printing shops and he used his savings to buy a hand press for printing stationery leaflets for friends and relations. He left home in 1940, at the age of 16, without much education, but went on to attend weekend and evening art classes in London at Regent Street School, Bolt Court school of printing in Fleet Street, and Toynbee Hall in Aldgate.

His path to becoming an exponent of the new typography was not without its detours and elements of chance. In his mid-teens, he became increasingly interested in painting and drawing and this had become a strong preoccupation by 1942, when he volunteered for the Royal Air Force (RAF). While waiting to be called up, he took a job with the advertising agent Cecil D. Notley and realized his knowledge of type was an asset. In the RAF, he worked in a Photo Interpretation unit as a cartographer. He was stationed near Marlow, Buckinghamshire, where he rented a cottage, read about Van Gogh and painted landscapes during the day.

It was Spencer's intention to continue painting after the Second World War. To support himself, he took a job in 1946 with a group called London Typographical Designers (LTD), founded by Leon French and William Morgan, who had worked as typographers during the war at the Ministry of Information. It was a full-time commitment and he soon stopped painting. LTD, the first typographical office of its kind, dealt with commercial printing, and Spencer designed trademarks – his Marconi trademark was still in use in 1980 – stationery ranges, catalogues and brochures. As his typographical ideas developed, he realized they were at odds with classical, symmetrical solutions and the 'new traditionalism' favoured by French and Morgan.[16]

In 1948, Spencer took a considerable risk and decided to become a freelance designer, a course of action then almost unknown.[17] He designed printed material and a monthly magazine for the

Above: *Typography*, no. 3, summer 1937. Spread from Jan Tschichold's article on type mixtures, showing two examples of his work. Publisher: Shenval Press.
Left: *Typography*, no. 5, spring 1938, 278 × 228 mm. Design: Robert Harling.
Below right: Spencer by *Punch* cartoonist Maurice Pownall, 1944.

14

5 TYPOGRAPHY

Typography: a quarterly published by the Shenval Press

Two Shillings · Spring 1938

Linguists' Club in Grosvenor Place, London. He also taught at the Anglo French Art Centre in St John's Wood, London, where the principal, Alfred Rozelaar Green, invited him to start a course in typography. In the post-war years, Green had transformed the old St John's Wood art school into a cultural centre and 'free academy' by putting on exhibitions and recitals and inviting international art-world celebrities such as Fernand Léger, Oscar Dominguez and Tristan Tzara to lecture and give tutorials.[18] A prospectus written and designed by Spencer explains his six-month course's intention,

> . . . to encourage, through experiment and wide research, the production and appreciation of work that is in harmony with the conditions of our time. It will avoid the imitation or creation of any style and will seek to prove that a dance ticket or trade-card can be a true expression of the art of typography no less than a limited edition.[19]

This small but confident announcement, in which some of Spencer's mature typographic concerns are already apparent, came to the attention of Eric C. Gregory – also known as Peter – chairman of Lund Humphries, who wrote to Spencer suggesting a meeting. Gregory was a founder, with Herbert Read and Roland Penrose, of London's Institute of Contemporary Arts (ICA). In January 1948, he asked Spencer to design the catalogue and other graphics for the ICA's first exhibition, 'Forty Years of Modern Art: 1907–1947'.

What set Spencer apart from most of his contemporaries in typography and design was his international outlook. In art classes, he mixed with German refugees. Many of his friends and associates in the RAF came from abroad; in Germany, in the final months of the war, he was most closely associated with Austrians and Czechs. He also absorbed European influences through his reading. When he was 16, a cousin gave him a copy of *Printing Design and Layout* by Vincent Steer. Spencer subsequently sold it in London's Charing Cross Road, then, in an act of symbolic exchange, went to nearby Zwemmer's bookshop and bought the Museum of Modern Art's *Bauhaus 1919–1928* (1938). He has often spoken of the importance for him of Robert Harling's and James Shand's *Typography* (1936–9). Jan Tschichold's article on 'Type mixtures', in the third issue, had a decisive influence on his eventual direction.[20] In his early 20s, Spencer admired the work

Right: Cover of prospectus for Spencer's typographic course at the Anglo French Art Centre, London, c. 1947, 102 x 127 mm. Design: Spencer.
Below: Front and back cover of leaflet for the Institute of Contemporary Arts, London, c. 1948, 191 x 331 mm. Design: Spencer.
Below right: Cover of leaflet advertising *Designers in Britain* 4, 1953, 194 x 133 mm. Design: Spencer.
Bottom: Catalogue cover for Common Ground, 1951, 215 x 138 mm. Design: Spencer.

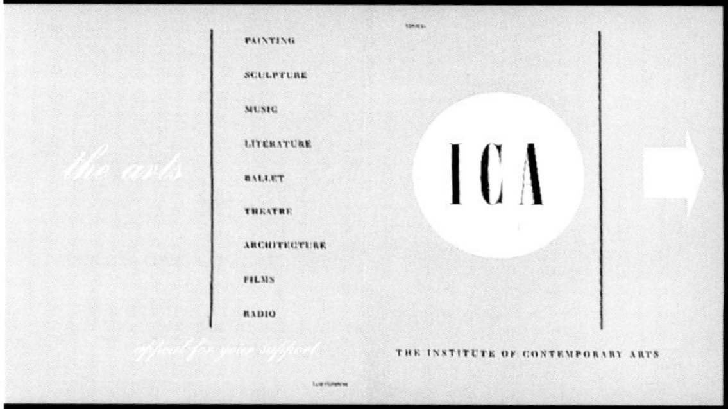

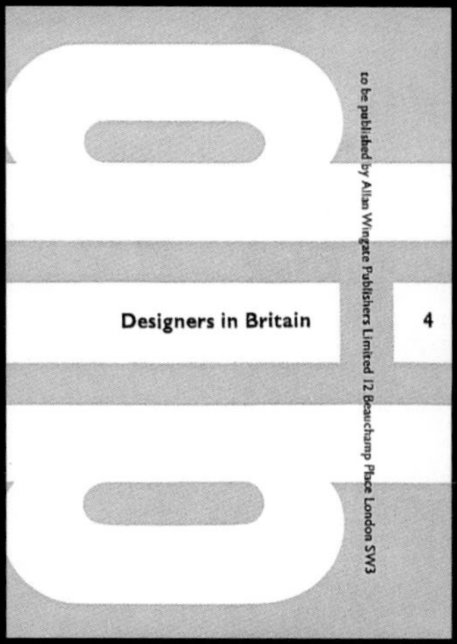

Above: *Typographica*,
OS no. 6, 1952, back
cover. Design: Spencer,
incorporating art by
the painter Vera Spencer,
then his wife.
Below: Spencer
and Marianne Mols,
London, 1953.

of H. N. Werkman and Willem Sandberg in The Netherlands, Max Huber in Italy and Pierre Faucheux in France, particularly for their use of different materials to give their work a three-dimensional character.[21]

In the decade after the war, Spencer's commercial success as a designer allowed him to travel widely in Europe. From September to October 1946, he visited Antwerp, Brussels and Paris; he returned to Paris the following April. In December 1948, he was in Lugarno, Lucerne and Zurich, and on this trip he met Imre Reiner and Max Bill for the first time. Trips to France, in 1949, and France and Spain, in August and September 1950, were followed, in June 1951, by visits to Milan, Berne, St Gallen and Zurich; in the course of the latter trip, Spencer met the Italian architect Ernesto Rogers, editor of *Domus* from 1946 to 1947; Rudolf Hostettler, then editor of *Schweizer Graphische Mitteilungen*; the Swiss typographer Max Caflisch; and Max Bill. In July and August of the same year, he returned to France and Italy. In January 1952, he was once again in Paris. In April and May 1953, on a trip to The Netherlands, Spencer visited the studios of many Dutch designers, among them Dick Ellfers, Wim Brusse, Otto Treumann, Benno Wissing and Alexander Verberne. In September, he went to Prague, Moscow, Leningrad, Tashkent and Tajikistan. In 1954, he returned to Switzerland. In 1955, he visited Israel, where he met the illustrator Josl Bergner. In May 1956, Spencer travelled to Belgium and The Netherlands, meeting Willem Sandberg and Naum Gabo. In December, back in The Netherlands, he visited Piet Zwart, and in May 1957, he was again in The Netherlands.

Spencer was attracted by the enthusiasm and outspokenness of the designers and artists he met on the Continent. In typographic terms, they seemed to him at least ten years ahead of their British counterparts. Although some of his contemporaries were moving in the right direction, he felt this was more by instinct than analysis; they were 'stumbling' rather than 'marching'. Moreover, Spencer's determined internationalism was reinforced by his two marriages, both to Europeans. His first wife, from 1945 to 1953, was Vera Singer, a Czech painter whom he met in the RAF.[22] In 1954, after their divorce, he married Marianne Mols, a Dutch national. She accompanied Spencer when he visited Piet Zwart in 1956, and acted as translator. Willem Sandberg and his

'THE PRINTER, IF HE IS TO ACCEPT RESPONSIBILITY FOR UTILITY PRINTING DESIGN, AS I BELIEVE HE SHOULD, MUST EMPLOY THE TYPOGRAPHER, NOT JUST AS A LUXURY RESERVED FOR "SPECIAL" JOBS, BUT AS THE PLANNER OF ALL PRINT.'

HERBERT SPENCER, 'FUNCTION & DESIGN IN BUSINESS PRINTING', 1950

wife became friendly with the Spencers and often made social visits to them in London.

The mood of insularity and nostalgia that pervaded large sections of the art and design communities in the years immediately following the Second World War is captured by an editorial statement in the journal *Alphabet and Image* (1946–8), Harling and Shand's successor to *Typography*: '... for the first five years of the existence of this magazine (on the *Image* side, at least), we shall reproduce only the work of artists of these islands.'[23] The complacent tone is characteristic of a publication which, in its first issue, had with some self-satisfaction offered a quaint image of the typographer 'stepping out of uniform back into his tweeds or morning coat', as though nothing fundamental had been changed by the war.[24]

For individuals of Spencer's generation and temperament, however, the Second World War was a great divide. In this period of temporary flux and confusion in society and the workplace, when, as *Typographica* contributor Michael Middleton explains, 'everything had been stirred up so much, the sediment hadn't settled, new formations and structures hadn't sorted themselves out', it was possible to build platforms and occupy positions that might have been inaccessible to all but the most privileged before the war.[25] In 1946, Middleton (b. 1917) became art critic of the *Spectator* in precisely this way; and so it was for Spencer:

> In the period after the war . . . anybody with real enthusiasm for a certain subject could generally manage to push it along. You had to

Above: Spencer at Moscow State University during a cultural tour of the USSR, 1953.

create the opportunities for yourself, but provided you brought enough enthusiasm to bear, almost anything was attainable. That's certainly true of the way I started *Typographica* in 1949.[26]

Spencer's post-war experiences as a typographer had rapidly brought him to the conclusion that there was a need for a new magazine. *Alphabet and Image* ceased publishing in December 1948 and, by sloughing off its typographic content, was metamorphosed into *Image* (1949–52). A second series of *Signature*, the pre-war journal of typography and the graphic arts, edited by Oliver Simon, began publishing in July 1946, but Spencer did not feel that it adequately addressed contemporary needs.[27] The experience of teaching at the Anglo French Art Centre had obliged him to start the process of formulating a coherent set of principles to underpin and inspire business design. His two years with London Typographical Designers had given him a sense of what these should *not* be. He had a strong conviction that his new magazine had a role, but at the time he started he 'hadn't really defined clearly what the objectives were', beyond the need to encourage a dialogue between designers.[28]

In the summer of 1948, Spencer was invited by the publisher George Weidenfeld to become consultant art editor of *Contact*, a literary and cultural magazine, and though this was only a brief episode, seeing its small staff gave him a sense of the relative ease with which a regular publication could be assembled. Undaunted by his lack of commercial and publishing experience, Spencer produced a dummy for *Typographica*, made arrangements with a printer, and only then began to think about problems of distribution:

> I went to Peter Gregory, who was the only person I knew at that time who could have helped me, and told him – in the way one does when one is 24 – that I was going to publish this magazine, and that I wanted him to distribute it. He said: 'My boy, you're going to lose a lot of money. I'll publish it for you.' It was typical of the man that he didn't say: 'let me think about this; come back tomorrow', but made an immediate decision – and that he and the firm stuck by it for 18 years.[29]

The early years of *Typographica* were a time of rapid professional development for Spencer. In the autumn of 1949, soon after the appearance of the first issue, Jesse Collins, head of the Graphic Design Department at London's Central School of Arts and Crafts, invited him to become a visiting lecturer. Spencer continued to teach at the school until 1955 and his students included Colin Forbes, Alan Fletcher, Ken Garland, Philip Thompson and Derek Birdsall. This consolidation of his earlier teaching experience intensified Spencer's need to formulate principles for typographic practice. Anthony Froshaug (1920–84) also taught typography at the Central School, in the late 1940s and early 1950s, and former students invariably contrast their styles as personalities and teachers. Froshaug was outspoken; Spencer was diffident. Froshaug was abrasive, an irritant; Spencer was gentle and kind. Froshaug ranged widely in his conversation and ideas; Spencer concentrated intensely

17

on the matter at hand. Froshaug was a purist who regarded working for business as 'selling out'; Spencer embraced commerce, offering students a tremendous example of what could be achieved. Froshaug socialized with his students; Spencer maintained his distance, did his teaching and departed promptly to get on with his other work. Froshaug was a free spirit, a 'poet'; Spencer exemplified the virtues of application and discipline.[30]

Yet the picture that emerges from descriptions of Spencer and Froshaug as contrasting personalities does not account for the aesthetic and intellectual richness of Spencer's taste, interests and thinking in his concurrent pursuit as editor of *Typographica*. Perhaps as a result of his deep reluctance to bang the drum on his own behalf, his practice often seems to exceed what he himself had to say about it.

In the early 1950s, though, while his typographic ideas were evolving, Spencer *was* highly focused on the commercial applications of his developing typographic craft. His relationship with Gregory and Lund Humphries led to a steady stream of commissions from a company regarded as one of the most technically advanced and forward-looking printing firms in Europe. Lund Humphries had held a small exhibition of Jan Tschichold's work in Bedford Square, London, in 1935 and commissioned Tschichold to redesign its letterheading and to design a volume of *The Penrose Annual*. Ruari McLean was employed by Lund Humphries' Country Press printing works in Bradford, Yorkshire, in the late 1930s, and after the war, Froshaug

also worked (although rather unhappily) as a freelance for the firm.

In January 1950, on the initiative of Anthony Bell, Gregory's assistant, Spencer was formally engaged as typographical consultant to Lund Humphries, a commitment that necessitated his presence at the Country Press for several days each month. It was a role that required diplomacy and tact. The idea that a designer should specify type was new to the British printing industry and far from welcome in most composing rooms. Even at Lund Humphries, an unusually enlightened printer in typographical terms, there was a need to win over the composing room by degrees; Spencer's predecessor had not lasted long. Spencer began by examining the wide range of typefaces held in the composing room and removing all those he did not consider compatible with good typography. He then drew up a set of rules for compositors that covered both 'jobbing' printing as well as book work, which was published in 1951 as *House Rules* 'for the guidance of compositors' at the press. His recommendation that Lund Humphries employ an authoritative composing room 'typographical editor', responsible for all matters of detail, was also taken up.[31]

This period of intensive typographic research and development led, in 1952, at the age of 28, to the publication of Spencer's first book, *Design in Business Printing*. He had a growing sense of an emerging audience of like-minded, self-aware young designers whose assumptions about typography were very different from those of the traditionalists within the printing industry. Spencer had first sketched out some of the book's concerns in 'Function & design in business printing', a short article in *Typographica*'s third issue, illustrated with examples of his own work.[32] A key theme is the flexibility of asymmetrical layout for both utility printing (items intended to inform) and publicity printing (items intended to advertise). Following the model of Tschichold's *Typographische Gestaltung*, the book is divided into two parts: a section on the development of modernist typography, from the Great Exhibition in 1851 to Tschichold's letterheadings, followed by a longer section offering detailed practical advice on type and paper, punctuation, figures and dates, the line, the paragraph, the page, tabular matter, footnotes, the importance of detail, and so on. Central to Spencer's argument, once again,

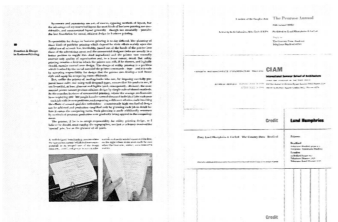

Above: *Typographica*, OS no. 3, 1950. Spread from Spencer's article 'Function & design in business printing', showing examples of his commercial work, including a credit note for Lund Humphries. Right: *Design in Business Printing* by Spencer, 1952, 254 × 186 mm. Design: Spencer. Publisher: Sylvan Press.

is his commitment to asymmetrical layout, which 'provides the best foundation for sound design in business printing'.[33]

As a polite but firm assault on the sacred cows of typographic tradition, the book was bound to cause a stir. Even *Design*, though sympathetic to Spencer as a rule, felt it necessary to caution that asymmetrical typography was not the answer to every design problem.[34] For others, *Design in Business Printing* became a standard reference work, and it was still being recommended by Ruari McLean, in 1992, in the revised edition of his *Manual of Typography*.[35]

By the mid-1950s, with nine or ten issues of *Typographica* behind him, with his book, his teaching position at the Central School, his Lund Humphries consultancy, and many other commissions, Spencer had attained a position of real influence.[36] 'Among the younger men, no name is better known,' observed *Printing Review* in 1953, in an article about an exhibition of Spencer's work at the Zwemmer Gallery, attended by colleagues such as Ashley Havinden of Crawfords advertising agency, Beatrice Warde of Monotype, Edward Wright, Theo Crosby and Anthony Froshaug.[37] In 1957, a printer's magazine initiated a 'Notable Typographers' column with another profile: 'His reputation and stature in the field of typography have brought him the respect and admiration of designers in Europe and America.'[38] Propelled into the design profession by his early discovery of printing, *Typographica*'s young editor was now the most prominent exponent of the new typography in Britain.

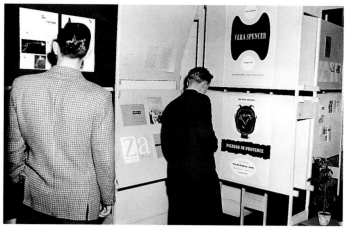

Above: Exhibition of Spencer's design work at the Zwemmer Gallery, London in October 1953. Below right: Spencer's house next to the Regent's Canal, 26 Blomfield Road, London, W9, 1959. Below left: Spencer in his office at Blomfield Road, 1959.

2.

The designer as editor

As an editor, Spencer enjoyed a degree of freedom to determine the content of his publication as great as if he had owned it himself. He could pursue his own interests wherever they led him, without interference from his publisher. *Typographica*, he observed, '… was very much a one-man operation. I wasn't really answerable to anyone. I suppose I just assumed that something which interested me – even if only marginally, at a certain level – would be of interest to others. If I'd had a committee, not to vet it but even to discuss it with, then probably some of these things would not have appeared … It was just a sort of enthusiasm for things and the fact that while the enthusiasm lasted I was able to publish something on the subject.'[1] There were other significant figures at Lund Humphries but most have died: Eric Gregory and his successor as chairman, Anthony Bell; Eric Humphries, managing director of the printing operation; Tom Scott, who oversaw the production of all 32 ≫→

Typographica, NS no. 9, June 1964. Design: Spencer. (Slightly larger than original.)

Typographica

Above: Front of folding leaflet advertising *Typographica*, with order form, 1962, 147 × 105 mm. Design: Spencer. The headline reads: 'Typographica Gathers Momentum'.

Below: Folding leaflet advertising *Typographica*, c. 1957, 152 × 558 mm. Design: Spencer. '*Typographica* is a stimulating, authoritative magazine – excitingly presented and abundantly illustrated – essential to all concerned with typography, design, and the graphic arts.'

issues; apart from Spencer, the only survivor with a close involvement is John Taylor, who joined the firm in 1959, after Gregory's death, and became publishing manager three years later. Piecing together *Typographica*'s publishing history is complicated by the fact that all administrative records on the printing side were lost in the course of the printer's liquidation in 1995, while the original publisher no longer exists. In 1976, the parent company sold its publishing assets to the London bookshop and publisher Zwemmer. Then, in 1985, the Lund Humphries imprint was acquired by Book Publishing Development. Taylor has no papers relating to *Typographica*'s production in his files and, like Spencer, he is certain that such material has not survived changes of ownership and address.

Throughout its 18-year life *Typographica* did not make a profit and it was evidently not expected to do so, as an announcement for the second series suggests:

> . . . although editorially we have been ambitious we have never sought to make profits and indeed every issue of *Typographica* has been heavily subsidized by printer and publisher, and by all our contributors and collaborators who have expended much time and effort in return for very modest rewards.[2]

Nevertheless, Lund Humphries gave Spencer complete support. The magazine never had a fixed budget, though he suspects that its managers kept 'half an eye' on the costs. Aware that it was an expensive investment, he refrained from being too demanding throughout the first series. The print specification for these 16

issues, with only an occasional use of special papers and insets, is markedly less elaborate than in the second series – simpler even than that of pre-war *Typography*. By the second series, Lund Humphries was sufficiently pleased with the response from readers for Spencer to feel free to specify – again without stated budgetary limitations – whatever printing effects he felt might be appropriate; insets, use of colour, and so on.

Exact figures for *Typographica*'s print run are one of the casualties of its lost records. Spencer remembers it as no more than 2,000 to 3,000 copies. Taylor suggests that, at least during the second series, it was 2,000, of which 1,500 would sell out fairly quickly, leaving 500 to 'trickle along'.[3] These figures are small by the standards of twenty-first century design publishing. International magazines of progressive inclination might print anything from 7,000 to 12,000 copies (the more populist American titles can achieve runs as high as 50,000). By mid-twentieth century standards, however, when graphic design as a profession was much less developed, with fewer potential readers, the figures are not especially low.

Relative smallness of circulation does not necessarily indicate lack of diffusion or influence. While precise information has been lost, internal evidence suggests the ambition of *Typographica*'s publishing programme. An editorial in the seventh issue notes with some jubilation that an analysis of records has revealed subscribers in more than 25 countries outside the UK, including Cuba, Egypt, India, Pakistan, Russia, Poland, Portugal, Japan, Israel, USA, Germany, Switzerland, France, Norway, Denmark, Canada, Australia, New Zealand, South Africa, Belgium and Sweden.[4] No figures are given, however, nor is anything said about who the readers might be. Further evidence of *Typographica*'s international distribution comes in a list of overseas agents first published in the same issue and regularly updated thereafter. It shows agents in Melbourne, Sydney, Vienna, Brussels, São Paulo, Toronto, Mexico, Copenhagen, Paris, Athens, Amsterdam, Milan, Tokyo, Auckland, Oslo, Cape Town and New York.[5] By 1962, the list had expanded to include booksellers in Buenos Aires, Cairo, Hong Kong, Calcutta, Tel Aviv, Lisbon, Salisbury (Rhodesia), Barcelona, Stockholm, Zurich, Istanbul and Chicago.[6]

The original plan was to publish *Typographica* every four months. In practice, its publication throughout the first series was irregular.[7] Other production commitments would sometimes take precedence at Lund Humphries, while Spencer himself was attempting to combine editing the magazine with his own practice. Some years only a single issue appeared. One of John Taylor's first tasks was to help put the magazine on a firmer footing. A statement in OS no. 16 announced *Typographica*'s intention to publish twice a year, on 1 June and 1 December, and throughout its second series the magazine stuck to this schedule.[8] Taylor believes that Lund Humphries continued to publish *Typographica* on this basis because it was a 'showcase' and 'very effective PR'; designers would see the magazine's quality of production and print and bring their business to the company.

By 1963, the year that Spencer was appointed editor of Lund Humphries' *The Penrose Annual*, the company had begun to consider closing the title, according to its chairman, Anthony Bell:

> Truth to tell, the thought of ending the *Typographica* series began to loom up when we were lucky enough to persuade Herbert to take over *Penrose*, which really had a great need for his flair. Herbert persuaded us, without great difficulty, to continue *Typographica* for a given further spell as there were quite a few things that needed to be said.[9]

The reason for closure given in the penultimate issue is bluntly economic: 'During the past seven years the sales of *Typographica* have risen substantially – but unfortunately the costs of producing a magazine of this kind and to this standard have risen still more dramatically.'[10] The last three issues are thinner in content, have fewer pages and possess none of the insets that distinguish many of the earlier issues. Spencer, asked in 1981 why the magazine had closed, gave no details, but merely observed that 'there is a right time to end activities as well as to start them and I do not regret bringing *Typographica* to an end when I did'.[11] The timing was in any case fortuitous as it resulted – as if by plan – in two equal-sized series.

Spencer had many contacts in art, design, architecture and publishing, but he belonged to no group and espoused no cause. By both temperament and strategy, he straddled two worlds: tradition and modernity. He was critical of an earlier generation, and rejected its typographic assumptions, yet he retained, as an editor, a fascination with much that a stricter modernist would

23

The Penrose Annual, vol. 60, 1967, 303 x 220 mm. Edited by Spencer. Design: Spencer.

have spurned. As a designer struggling to find ways to apply new typographic approaches in the wary design climate of early 1950s Britain, Spencer could see no point in provoking a 'head-on clash'. He contrasts his approach with that of Max Bill (1908–94), a powerful typographic influence on his own work. In Switzerland, Bill was 'anathema to most people in the printing field', notes Spencer, and alienated many, despite the high standard, consistency and logic of his work.[12]

The two key components, then, of Spencer's editorial approach were eclecticism, in regard to *Typographica*'s content, and pragmatism, in regard to its audience. Without an eclectic view of his subject matter, he could never have found sufficient material to sustain the magazine for 32 issues and 18 years. Art and design journals of more focused (or restricted) editorial philosophy, such as the extraordinary – and entirely lower case – Swiss concrete art and poetry publication *Spirale*, started by Marcel Wyss, Diter Rot and Eugen Gomringer, effectively fulfil a 'manifesto' function for their creators and adherents, but perhaps because they burn so brightly, can rarely be sustained. As editorial creations, they are subject to the same entropic process as the groups and movements they serve. *Spirale* lasted from 1953 to 1964, but stretched to only nine issues, with intervals of anything up to four years between them; at such a frequency it can no longer be properly classed as a 'magazine'.[13]

Without an informed and pragmatic awareness of his audience's interests, tastes, inclinations and prejudices, Spencer

Above: *Typographica*, OS no. 14, 1958. Spread from 'The publications of Gaberbocchus Press' by Spencer.
Below: Stefan Themerson, writer and co-founder of Gaberbocchus Press, c.1968.

could not have carried his readers with him for so long. His early readership, as contemporary reviews indicate, was a mixture of subscribers and buyers from traditional printing backgrounds and a smaller group of younger, progressively-minded designers like himself. This audience did not, he suggests, change fundamentally in character and composition as the first series progressed so much as 'expand enormously'. Non-traditional subjects would be tolerated as part of a balanced editorial mix, but not welcomed. By the late 1950s, and certainly by the early issues of the second series, Spencer was much more confident of the potential interest of the less conventional material to a new generation of art school-trained typographers, though such readers would still perhaps amount to only a minority of the total readership.[14] Before their introduction in *Typographica*, multidisciplinary artists such as Diter Rot and the Themersons were known to only a small circle of enthusiasts in Britain.

When it came to generating ideas and commissioning articles for *Typographica*, Spencer's approach was to be as open, flexible and responsive as possible:

> Of course, people came to me with all sorts of suggestions, many of which I didn't pursue, but I wasn't thinking up everything that appeared there. Very often something would develop out of a casual conversation and one would see it had possibilities and ought to be published.[15]

Ken Garland (b. 1929), who wrote about typophoto at Spencer's suggestion, describes Spencer as a 'magpie' in his search for arresting editorial material:

> Herbert was always ready to grab anything that was happening anywhere else. When I went to Switzerland for a couple of months and came back with a lot of stuff in 1960 . . . Herbert said, 'Ken, write an article.' So I wrote 'Typophoto' and I brought him a whole lot of stuff, mainly from people like Karl Gerstner, but also a lot of other material and Herbert lapped it up. He really had a great sort of journalistic thirst.[16]

On other occasions, a designer or writer with a particular enthusiasm would propose an article, as did Alan Bartram after discovering the work of Italian painter, graphic designer and photographer Franco Grignani. Spencer readily agreed.[17] Such a combination of strategies for generating material – by idea, by discovery and by proposal – is typical editorial practice. In addition, like many editors of small magazines, Spencer would sometimes, having identified a subject, choose to write about it himself.

As a self-taught copy-editor, he also undertook all the sub-editing. Some articles, by experienced writers, did not require much editorial attention at all. Surviving handwritten manuscripts, with the authors' crossings out and other amendments, by Nicolete Gray, for an article on the Civic Trust, and by Charles Hasler, for an article on printers' stock blocks, are virtually unchanged in their printed form, except for the insertion of additional punctuation marks and their rendering into *Typographica*'s editorial and typographic house style. Even the authors' titles remain as given. The articles would have been typed, then marked up, before being passed to Lund Humphries'

composing room, though the typed versions and galley proofs do not survive. On other occasions, particularly during the second series, some contributors had little or no experience of writing and considerable work by Spencer was required to put their rough drafts into fluent English. This was especially likely to be the case with first-time and foreign contributors to *Typographica*. The typewritten manuscript of an article on the Swiss-Italian designer Max Huber, written and signed by Antonio Boggeri, has been heavily edited by Spencer, with many deletions and insertions and no sentence left unchanged.

Spencer's eclecticism as an editor became more purposeful as he gained in experience. Throughout the first series, he recalls, he was 'flying by the seat of my pants'. He was also learning the craft of editing. A feeling for how a magazine's never entirely predictable component parts will mesh to make the whole can only be developed over time, with repeated try-outs, misfires and recalibrations. *Typographica*'s irregularity necessarily slowed this process down. Spencer had a general direction without being certain of exactly where he wanted to take his magazine. The articles dealing with abstract painting or French book illustration in the first series give *Typographica* editorial variety and visual interest without amounting to a concerted statement or programme for bringing together art and design. Of the painting, Spencer says: 'I felt it was interesting to show, though one wasn't quite sure where it was really leading.' Similarly, he published W. J. Strachan's series of articles on French illustration because

Ken Garland, designer, 1959

Typographica, OS no. 4, 1951. Opening spread from 'First principles and last hopes' by Toni del Renzio.

First Principles and Last Hopes

Lynn Chadwick: Drawing for mobile

TONI DEL RENZIO

15

First Principles and Last Hopes

LEFT: Victor Pasmore
BELOW, LEFT: Robert Adams
BELOW, RIGHT: Eduardo Paolozzi

they were 'interesting to see', even though they did not 'fit in with any philosophy of mine'.[18]

By the second series, Spencer had thoroughly learned the craft of editing. With greater confidence, he became more focused and selective. Now that he was exploring territory he had already mapped to some degree, editorial decisions could be made in a more conscious and deliberate way. Regular publication dates meant that there was a need to plan two or three issues ahead. Increasingly, he began to consider *Typographica* as a 'three-dimensional' progression, taking into account not only the balance of elements within an issue, but also an issue's position in the series and its relationship to the others. Instead of being reactive, leaving an issue open until close to publication, waiting to see what turned up, then publishing it if it interested him, he would make lists of topics and areas he wanted to cover (always allowing for the possibility of late changes to plan). This resulted in some even more striking contrasts of editorial and visual content than he had achieved in the first series. The main difference was that they were part of a more considered and complex mix, which achieved coherence in diversity. Each of *Typographica*'s most characteristic strands – modernist history, printing history, new typography, avant-garde experimentation and photography – developed over time and they were interwoven from issue to issue so that, with varying degrees of emphasis, each *Typographica* was representative of the series as a whole.

Ultimately, though, it is misleading to attempt to separate *Typographica*'s editorial content from its visual content and design presentation. The unity of these elements is a product of their interaction and this relationship is especially difficult to disentangle when editorial and design decisions are made in tandem by a single controlling sensibility and intelligence.[19]

Both series of *Typographica* got off to false starts and in each case it took Spencer two or three issues to settle on a design, which then remained unchanged for the rest of the series. Despite a provocative reference to the Bauhaus in his opening editorial, *Typographica*'s first issue is typographically conventional and even subdued. Spencer, perhaps following the two-column format of *Typography*, divided a generous page size of 310 x 236 mm into two equal 21 pica em columns separated by a 2-em gutter. The text, Monotype Walbaum no. 374, is set fairly solid – 10 on 12 point – giving a heavy-looking page when unillustrated. Evidently dissatisfied, he made some immediate adjustments with the second issue.[20] Again perhaps inspired by *Typography*, he varied the type style for each of the headlines – an article on copper-plate script employs a script – and introduced standfirsts justified to the full width of the measure (*Typography*, too, had made use of copy-fitted standfirsts). For an article on 'visual aids', he also broke with the established text grid. The effect was livelier, but lacked coherence both as a way of integrating type and illustration within articles, and in the relationship of the articles to each other.

With the simplifications of the third issue, Spencer achieved a clarity and durability of design equal to the clarifying arguments made in his article 'Function & design in business printing', published in the same issue. The overall text measure of 44 ems remained the same, but the static central axis of the previous two-column grid was avoided by dividing the measure into a main text column of 33 ems, leaving 11 ems for the folios and running heads (aligned with the first line of the article) and for illustrations which required more space than the text area alone. The Walbaum text type was increased in size to 11 point on 14 points of leading, and this combined with the wide margins to make a lighter, more elegant, less daunting page. When needed –

26

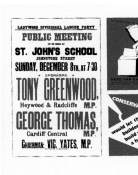

as it was in the third issue for an article on photograms – the 33-em column could be subdivided into two 16-em columns, giving a more flexible and dynamic three-column layout. Headlines and bylines followed a standardized style, ensuring a greater impression of unity throughout, and standfirsts were abandoned for good.

Typographica's typography needed no further modification at this point, but as the first series progressed, Spencer discovered a problem. The comparatively large page size, which had at first seemed an advantage, meant that typographic illustrations sometimes had to be given an entire page, which was wasteful, or to be reduced, sometimes uncomfortably, so that four would fit on a page. The second series presented an opportunity to reconsider this. Another reason for changing *Typographica*'s dimensions was that the large page size could be handled by only one of Lund Humphries' presses, if it were not to be printed uneconomically, and this often meant waiting until that press was free. The new page size – 272 x 210 mm – would not only accommodate illustrations more logically, but could be printed by several presses. As a non-standard paper size, it was nevertheless criticized by advocates of standardization.[21] A final advantage, from Spencer's point of view, was that the number of pages in an issue could be increased by roughly a half to at least 64. Spencer found the thinness and floppiness of the first series unaesthetic.

Despite this fundamental change, the first two issues of the new series look back to the first series – and the previous decade – in some crucial respects. Spencer changed the main text typeface from Walbaum to another serif typeface, Monotype Bembo no. 270, but in terms of overall typographic disposition the page is much the same: a broad, booklike (30-em) column of justified text, surrounded by generous margins. The furthest extent of the picture and caption area is once again marked by folios lining

Top: *Typographica*, OS no. 1, 1949. Spread from 'The integration of photo and type' by Charles Hale.
Centre: *Typographica*, OS no. 2, 1950. Opening spread from 'Political typography' by Michael Middleton.
Above: *Typographica*, OS no. 3, 1951. Opening spread from 'The possibilities of the photogram' by Michael Middleton.

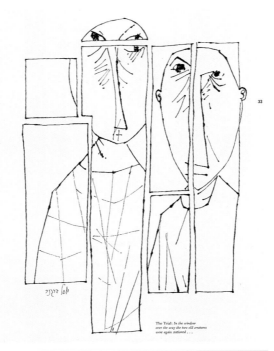

Top: *Typographica*, NS no. 1,
June 1960. Opening spread
from 'Yosl Bergner's
drawings to Kafka' by
Penuel Peter Kahane.
Above: *Typographica*,
NS no. 3, June 1961.
Opening spread from
'Typophoto' by Ken Garland,
showing a poster for
a furniture exhibition
by Celestino Piatti.

Typographica, NS no. 5,
June 1962. Opening spread
from 'Penguins on the
march' by Spencer.

with the start of the articles and ranged to just 1 ½ ems from the
fore edge. Only the titles, set in 24 point Monotype Grotesque
Series 216, fulfil the modernist promise of the new series
announcement in issue 16 – all of which, title and text, is set
unjustified in sanserif Monotype Grotesque Series 216. With the
third issue, Spencer set about rectifying this. The entire issue is
typeset in Monotype Grotesque Series 215 (regular) and 216 (bold).
The sanserif text is loosely line-spaced in 9 on 18 point Series 215,
giving an exceptionally open page, all text is unjustified and there
are no paragraph indents. Titles and bylines, occupying a single
line, are reduced, in the understated, 'objective' manner of Swiss
typography – seen in this issue in Ken Garland's 'Typophoto'
article – to the same size as the text. In a reversal of the previous
page design, Spencer moved the main text column out towards
the fore edge, reducing the fore edge margin and substantially
enlarging the central margins.

What remains unclear is why Spencer did not introduce these
changes a year earlier, in 1960, with the start of the new series,
since he had long been an advocate of unjustified setting. *Design
in Business Printing* contains a single unjustified text page inserted
quietly, without announcement, into the run of justified pages
to see whether the reader notices it – a striking example of the
stealthy pragmatism by which Spencer preferred to advance his
typographic cause.[22] One of his first acts, on becoming editor of *The
Penrose Annual*, in 1963, was to introduce unjustified setting: 'that
absolutely outraged people in the printing industry,' he recalls.

'A great many people did write and complain about that. They
thought it was monstrous.' By the third issue of *Typographica*'s
new series, he notes, 'I was in a strong enough position and I had
a sufficiently large following', to introduce unjustified setting; but
this would not have been possible, he felt, any earlier.[23] The delay
is best interpreted, perhaps, as an instance of his pragmatism.

The final adjustment to the new series' design came in the
fourth issue. By moving the folio to the foot of the page and
further reducing the fore edge margin, Spencer was able to enlarge
the main text measure to 29 ½ ems and fix the overall measure
at 45 ems. For the purposes of laying out pictures and captions,
this could be divided into three equal columns of 14 ems, with
1 ½ ems between them. The efficiency of the new grid, compared
to the first series, can be seen in one of Spencer's own articles, in
the fifth issue, where he was able to lay out Penguin book covers
six to a page.

In the second series, the balance of text and image in
Typographica shifted decisively and it became a much more
intensively visual publication. This was partly to do with the
possibilities of the new format, especially the extra pages, partly
a matter of Spencer's increasing confidence about Lund
Humphries' commitment to *Typographica* and his own growing
certainty about how he wanted it to develop. It was also a
necessary reaction to the nature and aptitudes of the magazine's
contributors, who were often designers, turning their hands to
writing, rather than experienced writers.

Below: *Typographica*, NS no. 10, December 1964. Spread from 'The compass rose' by W. E. May. The word 'rose' was used by maritime countries to refer to the figure on the face of a compass card.

Opposite: *Typographica*, NS no. 10. Spreads from 'Newspaper seals' by Allen Hutt. 'Seals' were small blocks of colour at the top of selected columns in broadsheet newspapers printed on a rotary press.

'THE NEWSPAPER SEAL HAS BEEN STRANGELY NEGLECTED BOTH AS A SUBJECT OF COMMENT AND OF CONSIDERATION. EVEN NEWSPAPERS WHICH HAVE GIVEN CAREFUL THOUGHT TO THEIR TYPOGRAPHY AND TO THEIR TITLE-PIECE SEEM OFTEN TO HAVE PAID SCANT REGARD TO THE DESIGN OF THE SEAL.'

HERBERT SPENCER, *TYPOGRAPHICA* EDITORIAL, 1964

Silk card for steering compass by West.
Mid nineteenth century.
Fleur-de-lis at north.
Decoration at east.
White points on black ground.

British naval card. About 1945. 6 in.
Fleur-de-lis at north, points at other cardinals only.
Letters at cardinal and half-cardinal points only.
Black card with white edge. Double set of degrees, one being reversed for observation in a prism.

French naval card, by E. Doignon. 1928.
8 in. Red star at north, letters at other cardinal and half-cardinal points.
Points and double set of degrees, the smaller one being reversed for observation in a prism.

United States naval card by Hand.
About 1940. 7½ in.
Fleur-de-lis at north and letters at remaining cardinal and half-cardinal points, which are the only points shown. Degrees.

Turkish card. 9½ in.
Star and crescent at north.
Arabic names for cardinal and half-cardinal points.
White points on black ground.

4

5

31

Here, left and right, is the complete range of seventeen seals used by the London *Evening Standard*, covering the normal run of editions from first to last and also providing suitable labels for the special occasion. The 'Late Special' and 'Late Extra' are, in fact, early and not late edition seals.

Below: The London *Evening News* believes in seal simplicity. For the final 'Night Special' the black overprint is in the forme.

A similar argument can be applied to those local weeklies of the larger sort which have a number of area editions; the seal can be an effective way of giving the edition its area or district label.

Even when the seal is used strictly as an edition indicator by an evening paper it can be given some decorative treatment. Examples are the various Final seals of the *Evening Standard*, each with its little blob of Eros, and the red-and-black Night Special of the *Evening News*. But however notions like these may be handled the central thing, with an edition seal, is to see that it does its job cleanly and well, that it is thought out in relation to the title-line and the overall arrangement of the title-piece. Plain type, that is to say a suitable arrangement of lettering with or without border, should not be disdained; but to maximize the colour available a reverse block treatment is both usual and common sense.

MONDAY, JULY 27, 1964 ● ● 3d. 55

n when we stood alone,
until victory was won'
E BY MPs
WINSTON

Two centuries for England

9

This detail, actual size, is from a mid-nineteenth century block cut in deal plank (the full block, 24 inches wide, is made up of three pieces). It was used in a provincial printing office – in Reading – and it is now in the St Bride Printing Library

42

Thorowgood c.1839

Two blocks from the S. & C. Stephenson sale catalogue of 1797 and one from Caslon & Livermore 1830

Davison c.1835, and
Caslon & Livermore 1830

44

Thorowgood c.1839

Thorowgood 1825   Caslon 1798 (above and below)

This Indenture,

45

In the first series, the more heavily illustrated pieces are the exception. Long runs of pages without text rarely occur. Exhaustively researched taxonomies, rhythmically organized on the page by Spencer for maximum visual impact, with dramatic changes of scale and use of special papers, did not become a regular feature until the second series. *Typographica*, NS no. 10, for instance, includes three such articles – on newspaper seals (ten pages), compass cards (18 pages) and printers' stock blocks (19 pages) – all intensively illustrated. The same issue concludes with a ten-page article on 'Sex and typography', about Robert Brownjohn's titles for the James Bond films *From Russia with Love* and *Goldfinger*, which has only a few hundred words of text and mostly consists of images.

The rich supply of visual material, orchestrated by Spencer with great sensitivity to aesthetic effect, was further enriched by the use of paper and insets. Here, again, the material qualities of the early *Typographica* recall some of the effects achieved pre-war at Shenval Press by Harling's *Typography*. *Typographica*'s letterpress printing on Basingwerk Parchment, which was smooth enough to take half-tone illustrations and receptive to type, was supplemented by colour sections printed by offset-litho, also used for printing the wrapper. Contrasts of glossier coated papers, lightweight and coloured papers and the uncoated Parchment are a feature from the start. As early as OS no. 4, Spencer included a throw-out inset in Strachan's article on the French illustrator Roger Chastel. OS no. 6 illustrates an article on printers' and

Opposite: *Typographica*, NS no. 10, December 1964. Two consecutive spreads from 'The emergence of the printer's stock block' by Charles Hasler.

Above: *Typographica*, OS no. 10, 1955. Spread from 'Stedelijk Museum catalogues' by Spencer. The right-hand page is a tip in of a Sandberg design, supplied by Druckerij C. A. Spin en Zoon, Amsterdam. Below: *Typographica*, OS no. 7, 1953. Spread from 'Newspaper typography' by Walter Tracy, with fold-out inset of *Le Figaro*, 300 × 430 mm.

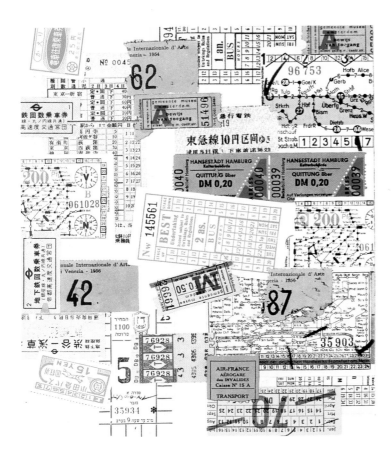

For the exhibition of W. J. H. B. Sandberg's work, posters were erected in the grounds at the rear of the de Jong gallery so that they could be viewed, as seen here, through the window.
The page opposite is from Sandberg's *Nu*, one of the series of Quadrat-Prints issued by de Jong & Company. *Nu* was published in 1959.

of the processes involved and to exploit the artistic possibilities of those processes. As the result of these invisible and anonymous but important activities of Brattinga many posters have been produced such as could never have originated in the artists' studios with the aid of brush, crayon, pen and pencil alone. No wonder that Brattinga's ideal is not to reproduce but to produce. This is the idea that holds the key to the central problem of machine aesthetics.

Another fruit of the contact which this printing office has established with the cultural world is the series of *Quadrat-Prints*. This publication, appearing at irregular intervals, is devoted to the fields of literature, plastic art, architecture, music and design. A sumptuous beginning with a series of photographs of one of the Dutch architect Rietveld's works was followed by issues on Chagall (incorporating a print specially lithographed by the artist), and the work of the American architect, Buckminster Fuller. A recent issue (NU) was written and designed by Sandberg and another by the modern Dutch composer Ton de Leeuw, entitled *Music and Technology*. Jan Bons's mural in Mexico City will be the subject of a forthcoming issue. The *Quadrat-Prints* are of course distributed free and Brattinga has further delighted his public now and then with fine lithographs published in the same format, and including a number of illustrations to the *Fables* of La Fontaine by the artist Timmer.

founders' type specimens with eight bound-in folded sheets. OS no. 7 has delicate newsprint insets from *Le Figaro* and *The New York Times*, as well as the Max Bill inset. An article on the Stedelijk Museum's catalogues in OS no. 10 includes a tip in of one of Sandberg's catalogue pages, printed on grainy sugar paper by an Amsterdam printer.

The composition of issues in the second series is even more elaborate. Four colour pages in *Typographica*, NS no. 2 were printed by de Jong and Company of Hilversum in The Netherlands – the subject of the article. The same issue has a four-page inset from Richard Hamilton's typographic version of Marcel Duchamp's *The Green Box*.[24] The smaller pages, set within the page frame of *Typographica*, become a book-within-a-book; Spencer's visual layering of Hamilton's interpretation of Duchamp's mechanistic diagrams on to Hamilton's typographic paste-up – printed on the *Typographica* page below – acts as a graphic analogy for the conceptual density of Duchamp's enigmatic masterpiece. A comparison with Theo Crosby's more routine handling of similar visual material in *Uppercase*, no. 2, for Hamilton's article 'Towards a typographical rendering of The Green Box', highlights the forensic care lavished by Spencer on *Typographica*'s aesthetic and material properties.[25] Crosby's layout is documentation; Spencer's is something more.

In the second series, in particular, Spencer was engaged as a designer in a continuous process of incorporation by which the graphic material he showed was, to varying degrees, assimilated

Typographica, NS no. 2, December 1960. Spread from 'de Jong, Hilversum' by B. Majorick. The left-hand page is from Sandberg's *Nu*, published in 1959.

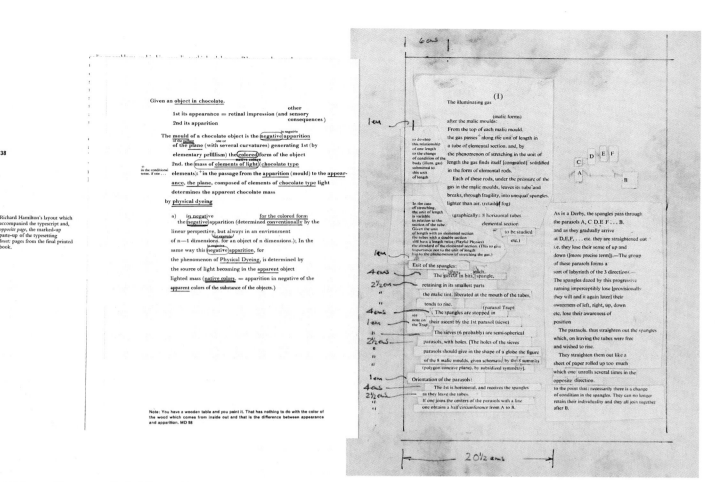

Above: *Typographica*,
NS no. 2, December 1960.
Spread from '"The Green
Box"' by Edward Wright,
a review of Richard
Hamilton's typographic
version of Marcel
Duchamp's notes for the
Large Glass. Typographica's
printer Lund Humphries
printed the book and
a four-page section is
included as an inset,
228 × 153 mm.
Right: *Uppercase*, no. 2,
1959, 175 × 263 mm.
Spread from 'Towards
a typographical rendering
of The Green Box' by
Richard Hamilton.
Publisher: Whitefriars.

Overleaf: *Typographica*,
NS no. 8, December 1963.
Spread from 'Concrete
poetry & Ian Hamilton
Finlay' by dom Sylvester
Houédard.

Poster poem by Ian Hamilton Finlay

on the right, a red blinker

le circus!!

smack

K47

they

leap

BARE-BACK

through

the

rainbow's

and crew

also

corks

nets

etc.

hoop

on the left, a green blinker

problem of the non & the non-non. Nonsemantic is even more concrete, more self-communicative. Overspill into EARVERSE (poésie à lire): sonorisms like f i sound poems invented by Hugo Ball 1915: n.1 gadgi beri bimba; Schwitters' beautiful priimiitittii (*transition* n.3): grim glim gnim bimbim (*mécano* 4–5 1923) & classical Primordial Sonata (Ursonate, based on Hausmann's *fmsbw*: 1924–33); or hans g helm's 'FA:M'AHNIESGWOW' structures developing this with stronger almost eyeverse typographic attention; all serial electronic music beginning early 50s at Radio Cologne (Stockhausen Boulez &c). Even Schwitters' **W** poem 1924 (began soft ended loud at 1st performance). EYEVERSE (poésie visuelle): like f i Francis Picabia's typographic poem-portrait of Tristan Tzara 1918, Diter Rot's *boks*, Japanese brush paintings, Alcopley's poetry without words, John Furnival's space elaborations, tornpaper doily-poems. Reduced to suprematist ultimate, *white on white*, & *poème blanc for ian hamilton finlay*.

Nonsemantic overspills further to f i total nature/art ambiguities of Kaprow's *Yard* & *Combines*; Rauschenberg's *Assemblages*; Dine's *Collages* & the Paris *New Realism*; New York *Happenings*; the Amsterdam *Dylaby* (dynamic labyrinths of Rauschenberg Raysse de Saint-Phalle Tinguely Ultveldt & Daniel Sporri himself a concretista); to current motorised painting & sculpture, mobile frescoes, sculptures sonores, pyromagnétiques, hydrauliques; lumino-dynamic creations lit from inside or outside; & true 3-d cinétisme plastique. All these: interart invasions, interpenetrations, coexistentialisms, mutual time-space interventions; kinetic, dynamic, spatial (cf useful survey of field work by Schöffer Malina Tinguely Calder Bury Le Parc Kosice Aubertin Takis Monari Vardenaga Boto & Hoenisch in UNESCO *Courier* September 1963) are concentric to nonsemantic concrete/spatial poetry: they are the background of pure concrete, the world of the 'création d'objets sonores poétiques ou visuels', a world where fauves & suprematists meet – in Scotland it is where they meet in a toymaker.

Ian Hamilton Finlay

Poet typographer toymaker – poetographer typographer toypographer – poetoypographer. As pure concrete poet Finlay is interested in contracting & constricting language into semantic economies: in purity. As typographer, in constructing these economies visually: at letting them create their space & move through it. As toymaker: in giving the thing its sense of the sacred, the unique, individual, irreplaceable, human, friendly. He makes ikon & logos one.

Hatred either of current age or dead dead past, of the *condition humaine*, of contingency & pressures – all that is implied & everytime in whatever is new. It needn't be expressed. It never is in Finlay. In a note he sent for this article: ' . . . so

into the grain of the page, in some cases quite literally, so that it became a partly recontextualized component in the evolving work that was *Typographica* itself. This was achieved, as a rule, by eliminating the distancing frame formed by the real material edge of the object being displayed. Lacking definite boundaries, its image could form a tighter visual bond with adjacent imagery and, ultimately, with the composite page – the page's edge became, in effect, its new boundary. Spencer subjected a wide range of graphic objects to this treatment, always achieving a considerable gain, in terms of his own page design's impact, as a result.

In an article on the American artist Alcopley, untitled abstract drawings in black ink, plus a few with colour washes, float across the capacious tank of the page. In a historical review of Polish Futurism, designs in red and black by Henryk Berlewi are reprinted actual size, but the original paper's edge is not shown, while the original backgrounds have been approximated by Spencer with a mustard-coloured sugar paper that gives the designs a semblance of unity they may not, in actuality, possess. In a further instance of graphic assimilation, a concrete *Poster Poem* by Ian Hamilton Finlay is rendered typographically. Spencer removed the poster-like border requested by Finlay, so that the page edge becomes the poem's border, and reversed Finlay's suggestion that the hoop be in colour; instead, the hoop is in black, the type in red. In a letter, Finlay responded warmly to the proofs Spencer sent him, 'especially of the poster poem, which is one of those lovely surprises – an idea actualized into something even

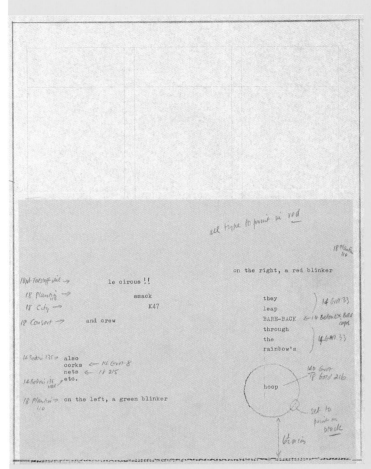

Above: Spencer's typographic mark-up for Ian Hamilton Finlay's *Poster Poem*, in *Typographica*, NS no. 8, 292 × 218 mm. (See page 36.)
Opposite: *Typographica*, NS no. 7, May 1963. Two consecutive spreads from 'Design underfoot' by Anthony Robinson, printed on rough sugar paper.

'I WOULD LIKE, IF I COULD, TO BRING INTO THIS, SOMEWHERE, THE UNFASHIONABLE NOTION OF "BEAUTY", WHICH I FIND COMPELLING AND IMMEDIATE, HOWEVER THEORETICALLY INADEQUATE. I MEAN THIS IN THE SIMPLEST WAY – THAT IF I WAS ASKED, "WHY DO YOU LIKE CONCRETE POETRY?" I COULD TRUTHFULLY ANSWER "BECAUSE IT IS BEAUTIFUL".'

IAN HAMILTON FINLAY, *BETWEEN POETRY AND PAINTING*, 1965

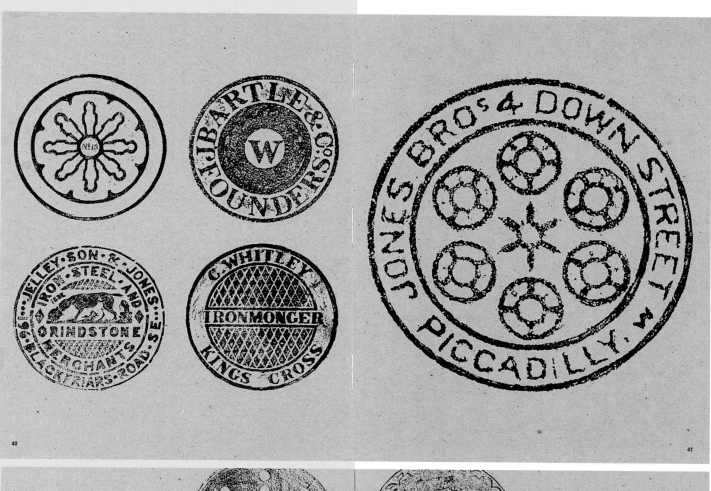

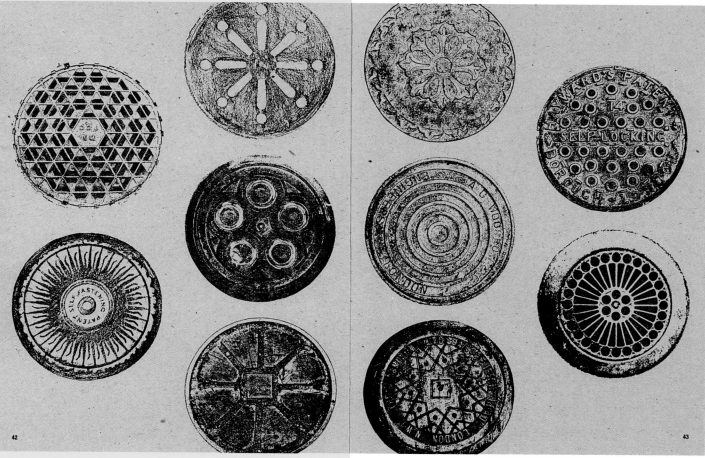

better than one had dreamed of...' He did, however, suggest that reinstating the border 'would make it just perfect'.[26] Spencer clearly did not agree.

'Design underfoot', an article on manhole covers, is one of the most extreme examples of the way in which graphic material is not simply incorporated by Spencer but almost sedimented into the page. It would have been possible to illustrate the subject by photographing covers *in situ* in the street. Instead, rubbings of the ornate discs are printed in flattening black outline on a rough grey-brown sugar paper. Spencer unfolds a captionless surface pattern, starting and ending with a single large cover and moving through a series of group variations. The subject matter is made visually arresting, using these techniques of graphic amplification, whether the reader finds it intrinsically interesting or not.

Spencer used a similiar approach in the first, large-format edition of *Pioneers of Modern Typography* and in the later revised edition, and the criticisms he received could equally be levelled at *Typographica*. Illustrations and blocks from the magazine were reused in the book. For Robin Kinross, reviewing *Pioneers*, such attempts at 'partial simulation' are misleading. Historians of graphic design agree that 'the edge of the sheet of paper or of the page must be shown (or, in a line image, reconstructed)'. Without this, the image 'leaks out of its planned frame and thus loses meaning: it becomes mere "design" in the sense of decorative pattern.'[27]

Spencer acknowledges the legitimacy of this criticism of *Pioneers*, though he does not believe that precise dimensions are necessary or appropriate in a magazine. In the case of *Typographica*, the effect that Kinross dismisses as 'mere "design"' – from his perspective as a historian – was Spencer's aim. Retaining all the borders around the illustrations would have made *Typographica* 'much more static and remote'. Spencer adds: 'I wanted to present things in – to use an abused word – an exciting way and so I often reproduced things in a size or in a way that creates an interesting magazine page.'[28] His intention was not literal reproduction, which if pursued to the limit would require nothing less than a full-size facsimile, so much as an evocation of the spirit and experience of the original piece.[29]

A more forgiving assessment of Spencer's integrationist approach as editor-designer is offered by Jasia Reichardt, a contributor to *Typographica*: in this respect, she observes, Spencer

 . . . was postmodern before his time. This is what postmodernism is, according to definition: that you absorb and re-create, no? . . . So it's a kind of formal collage, in a way, at least respecting the content, but not the way it looks. The look is interpreted, but the content is not changed.[30]

Breaking free from the sometimes deadening effects of sober art historical documentation, Spencer's interpretations unreservedly acknowledge their own highly contingent status as reproductions. An illustration of a piece of graphic design is not the original – however meticulously framed and labelled – any more than a painting of a pipe is a pipe.

106

H. N. Werkman.
Left: From *the next call* 4, 1924.
Opposite: This print, entitled *Compo...
with letter O*, was produced by Werkn...
in 1927.

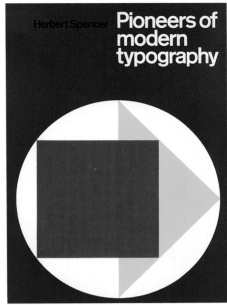

Above: *Pioneers of Modern Typography* by Spencer, 1969, 304 × 219 mm. Design: Spencer. Publisher: Lund Humphries.
Left: Spread from *Pioneers of Modern Typography*, showing prints ('druksels') created by H. N. Werkman in the 1920s.

Below: *Typographica*, OS no. 11, 1955. Opening spread from 'H. N. Werkman, printer-painter' by Spencer. The left-hand page is a tip in. The colour blocks were loaned by the Dutch printer S. Gouda Quint/ D. Brouwer en Zoon.

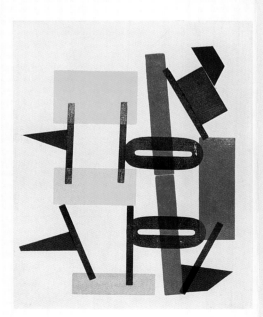

H. N. Werkman, printer-painter

by Herbert Spencer

19

Hendrik Nicolaas Werkman was an artist who made his livelihood as a printer and who used the materials and equipment available in a printing office to create many of his most interesting pictures.

Werkman was born in 1882, the son of a veterinary surgeon, and he lived all his life in Groningen in northern Holland. He began his career as a journalist and later took control of a large local printing office, but this business foundered during the economic crisis which followed the First World War. Werkman was able, however, to keep some type and a small amount of simple equipment and with this he established a workshop in the loft of a warehouse, where, with the aid of a single assistant, he maintained himself by printing the miscellaneous assortment of stationery, leaflets, and posters required of a small jobbing printer in a busy provincial and university town.

Werkman had produced his first painting in 1917, at the age of 35, and he had continued to paint at home in his spare time; but now, in 1925, installed in his new workshop, he began to explore the possibilities of utilizing in his pictures the materials which came readily to hand: printing ink, rollers, type. In order to distinguish these pictures from his oil paintings, Werkman called them *druksels*,[1] which means simply 'prints'. But although he made use of printing ink and hand-rollers, and sometimes of type, rules, and a hand-press, his technique had nothing in common with normal printing technique, concerned as that is with multiple production. These early pictures of the period 1925–5 are, however, nearer to normal printing technique than any of his later works and in them he made frequent use of printer's rule and odd letters of poster type – often using the backs of the wood-letters to produce rectangles of flat colour. Lightly printed on coarse paper, these early pictures are relatively subdued in colour. Many of Werkman's pictures of this period have unfortunately been lost or destroyed.

After these initial experiments, Werkman gradually developed his technique by making greater use of the hand-roller, first to roll flat colours direct onto the paper and, later, by using the edge of the roller to draw supple, sensitive lines. His pictures employing this technique are powerful and direct, but often they lack definition. Soon, however, Werkman discovered the *schablone* (stencil) and this was a development of fundamental importance to his technique. It enabled him to exercise in his compositions greater discipline of shape and form and he used this method with only minor variations throughout the rest of his life.

Werkman produced his stencils by cutting a sheet of paper with an old razor, which he used as quickly and freely as a pencil. Both parts of the sheet – the cut-out shape and the 'surround' – were utilized: first the ink (which was mixed on a palette) was rolled over the cut-out shape to produce a coloured background to a white silhouette, then the 'surround' was employed to fill in the silhouette with another colour. The order in which the colours were applied was of course of great

[1] The common word in Dutch for all printed matter is *drukken*. By describing his works as *druksels* Werkman stressed their experimental nature.

3.

Assimilating the avant-garde

There is an inescapable sense, reading the historical articles in
Typographica, that Spencer's commitment to publishing such
material lay mainly in the visual opportunities it afforded. Charles
Hasler's 'A show of hands', about printers' fists, in 1953, established
a standard of visual research and demonstrated a taste for taxonomy
that Spencer and his contributors would sustain for the rest of
Typographica's life. More than a hundred examples are shown. As is
usual with articles of this kind in the magazine, no explanation is
offered – either in the form of an editorial or as an introduction – for
the material's inclusion. Its interest for readers is simply assumed,
and given the revivalist concerns of the period, assumed with good
reason. Hasler ends his short survey by considering twentieth-
century fists and concludes that Eric Gill is the only important
designer to have paid them any attention. The article's gentle call
to action is unconvincing, however, because Hasler, despite the ⋙→

RIGHT: J. Oomkens J. Zoon, Groningen, 1807.

BELOW: Enschede, Haarlem, 1757.

BELOW RIGHT: Signs included in the sale catalogue of Abraham Elzevir's printing materials in 1713.

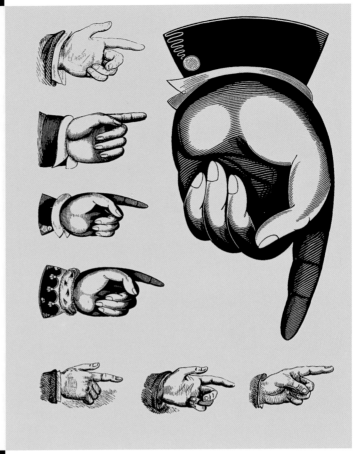

matter-of-fact and trady examples which are still to be found in most founders' and printers' specimen books.

Theatre and music-hall bills were a much used medium for the display of fists, especially if an artist of the fame of Charles Coborn were appearing. It was not unusual (particularly on provincial playbills) to find more than twenty different type faces and a row of half a dozen or more fists pointing downwards to the artist's name, with a coarse half-tone portrait thrown in for good measure. And some of the more decorative fists of the early part of the century were still enjoying quite a vigorous life in the nineties.

One nineteenth-century printer deserves mention because of the lively printing which he produced – Andrew White Tuer of the Leadenhall Press. Four fists are reproduced from his book 1,000 *Quaint Cuts from Books of other Days* and were most probably cut by Joseph Crawhall who produced a great quantity of woodcut material for the Press.

In our own day the only outstanding designer to turn his attention to the design of fists has been Eric Gill who produced some pleasant designs for the Monotype Corporation. His cuffed hand was used on the programme of the Conference of the Federation of Master Printers in 1928. This programme was an historic one, for in it Gill's sanserif type made its first appearance in printing, an event which caused a great deal of interest and controversy. Linotype also show some pleasant designs many of which are very much like those of the early nineteenth century. Among modern printers, Bruce Rogers achieved a fine effect in his *Fables of Æsop*, 1933, in which fists appear on the half title and colophon, and on the contents page to indicate which of the fables are illustrated.

Typographers today, especially those working for exhibitions, find that the range of fists available is very small and further that the range of outstandingly good ones is smaller still. If the fist is to re-establish its function in display typography, there is surely a need for some good contemporary designs.

ABOVE: The pica fists which formed part of Dr Fell's purchases from Holland for the Oxford University Press in the seventeenth century.

RIGHT: Four fists cut by Joseph Crawhall, in the chapbook style, for the Leadenhall Press in the late nineteenth century.

OPPOSITE PAGE: Plain and coroneted designs from Sharwood's huge specimen book of cast ornaments, c.1855.

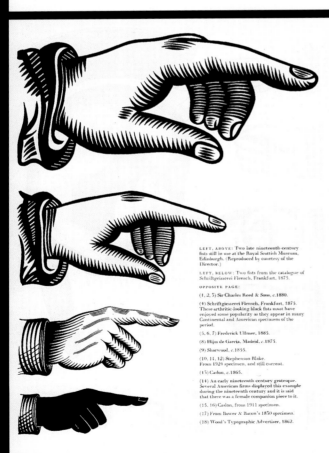

LEFT, ABOVE: Two late nineteenth-century fists still in use at the Royal Scottish Museum, Edinburgh. (Reproduced by courtesy of the Director.)

LEFT, BELOW: Two fists from the catalogue of Schriftgiesserei Flensch, Frankfurt, 1875.

OPPOSITE PAGE:

(1, 2, 5) Sir Charles Reed & Sons, c.1880.

(4) Schriftgiesserei Flensch, Frankfurt, 1875. These arthritic-looking black fists must have enjoyed some popularity as they appear in many Continental and American specimens of the period.

(5, 6, 7) Frederick Ullmer, 1885.

(8) Hijos de Garcia, Madrid, c.1875.

(9) Sharwood, c.1855.

(10, 11, 12) Stephenson Blake. From 1924 specimen, and still current.

(15) Caslon, c.1865.

(14) An early nineteenth century grotesque. Several American firms displayed this example during the nineteenth century and it is said that there was a female companion piece to it.

(15, 16) Caslon, from 1911 specimen.

(17) From Bower & Bacon's 1830 specimen.

(18) Wood's Typographic Advertiser, 1862.

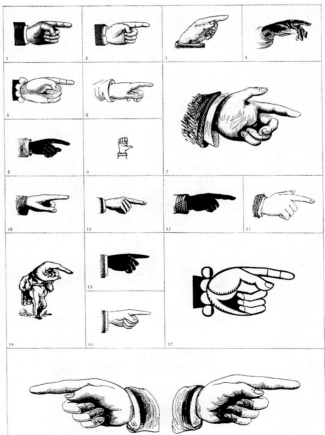

charm of his subject, has not demonstrated a pressing contemporary need for the perpetuation of the printers' fist.

If *Typographica*'s writers on pre-twentieth century printing, lettering and typography make few attempts to discuss their interests in terms of present-day needs and developments, this is only to be expected of an essentially backward-looking conception of design. Spencer himself is for the most part silent on these subjects: content to show, rather than tell. Early twentieth-century graphic design and typography, always a vigorous presence in *Typographica*, is another matter. On this subject, Spencer is much more explicit, both in the magazine and elsewhere, about his beliefs and intentions in publishing such material. He may have had a foot in both worlds, but the direction of travel was from the old to the new.

By the mid-1930s, the new typography identified with such figures as El Lissitzky, Kurt Schwitters, László Moholy-Nagy, Jan Tschichold and others had begun to make an impression in Britain. Of these 'pioneers of modern typography' – to use Spencer's Pevsnerian phrase – Tschichold was the most significant in British terms. Unlike the artist-typographers, whose typography was crude, Tschichold had a full command of print specification and printing and he was also an articulate theorist of his own practice.[1] In the early 1930s, he wrote several articles for *Commercial Art* introducing modernist ideas about typography, photography and exhibition display.[2] In 1935, his work was exhibited at Lund Humphries' London offices in Bedford Square. Two years later, he published the *Typography* article on type mixtures that was to be an important early influence on Spencer.[3] In 1937, too, his concise reflections on the new typography were included in *Circle*, the international survey of constructive art:

> . . . we consider the use of ornament and rules in the manner of earlier styles as disturbing and contrary to the contemporary spirit. The form should arise clearly and unequivocally out of the requirements of the text and pictures only, and according to the functions of the printed matter.[4]

The drive of the new typographer, he continued, must be 'towards purification and towards simplicity and the clarity of means'.

At a time when the rediscovery of Victoriana was gathering momentum, such ideas were received with little enthusiasm. Robert Harling, reviewing Tschichold's *Typographische Gestaltung* in 1937, suggests that any typographer, whether he can read German or not, should possess a copy 'so that occasionally he can turn through its cleansing, clinical pages' before reminding himself of alternative aesthetic possibilities by consulting Francis Meynell's Nonesuch books, or Ashley Havinden's advertisements.[5] Twelve years later, in an editorial in *Image* denouncing the 'cult of the seamless and the streamlined', Harling informs his readers, with the finality of someone washing his hands of the matter, that 'Herr Tschichold and his functional asymmetry were really too refrigerated and mathematical to be true', before going on to excoriate 'aesthetic totalitarianism' and the 'aridity of mechanical functionalism'.[6]

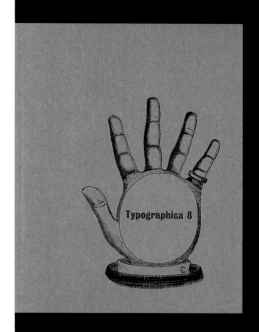

Opposite: *Typographica*,
OS no. 8, 1953.
Consecutive spreads from
'A show of hands' by
Charles Hasler.
Top: *Typographica*,
OS no. 8. Design: Spencer.
Above: *Ark*, no. 4, February
1952, 180 × 239 mm.
Design: David Gentleman.
Publisher: The Royal College
of Art, London.

The considerable reluctance of a nostalgia-dominated post-war design establishment to engage with the typographic ideas of Tschichold and other new typographers can be gauged from the handbook *Graphic Design* by John Lewis and fellow RCA tutor John Brinkley, published in 1954.[7] In a lengthy, detailed and in some respects well-researched study, many respectful pages are devoted to British illustrator-designers such as Paul Nash, Eric Ravilious, Edward Bawden and Lynton Lamb, while Tschichold rates not a single mention and the Bauhaus is accorded just three patronising and dismissive paragraphs.

Such was the context in which *Typographica*'s earliest issues appeared. In a carefully worded editorial in his first issue, Spencer made plain the magazine's commitment to the modern:

> Typography is not an independent Art: it is a means to an end, not an end in itself. It must always be subservient to the text which is its *raison d'être*. The text cannot be regarded merely as a point of departure for an experiment in aesthetics. The typographer's personal contribution will depend upon, and must be limited by, his ability to translate the writer's message into a form which is both intelligible and appropriate.

> New forms evolve out of the old in answer to new needs, and as a result of new methods and materials. Modern typography is a development of traditional typography – and the Bauhaus is now as much a part of our tradition as Baskerville and Bodoni. We cannot equal the great typography of the past by imitation; but by fully understanding contemporary problems, by carefully examining the best solutions to the problems of the past, by having a definite objective in all our

experiments and avoiding mere innovation, and by fully exploiting the means, the materials, and the machines at our disposal, we shall make our own real contribution to the development of the Art of Typography.

> The first purpose of *Typographica* will be to present serious analyses of various aspects – aesthetic and technical – of contemporary typography; it will also show, and comment upon, typographical experiments of significance, and provide a medium for the examination and discussion of contemporary problems.[8]

Understated as this might now seem, Spencer's equation of the Bauhaus with Baskerville and Bodoni was a forthright statement of principle. Only the most progressive and internationally-minded of his British readers would have regarded the German design school, in 1949, as part of their own 'tradition'. Sure enough, as Spencer recalled in 1967, the 'brief reference to the Bauhaus in that introduction provoked an indignant response from some eminent guardians of the printed word'.[9] Spencer's emphasis on the 'contemporary' in this passage and his commitment to 'experiments' and the 'new' emerge with conviction, despite the cautionary note sounded by the opening paragraph. Less clear is what he means by 'mere innovation'. However well defined the objective, the outcome of any experimentation is necessarily uncertain, while innovation suggests, if anything, successful experimentation productively applied. It is a small early sign, perhaps, of the tensions inherent in a support for the experimental within the context of commercial communication

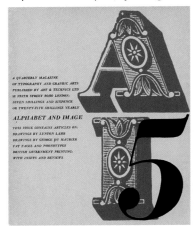

Above: *Alphabet and Image*, no. 5, September 1947, 246 × 197 mm. Design: Robert Harling. Publisher: James Shand (Art & Technics).
Right: *Typographica*, OS no. 3, 1950. Design: Spencer.

Opposite top: *Typographica*, OS no. 14, 1958. Opening spread from 'Old-fashioned types and new-fangled typography' by Alan Fern.
Opposite bottom: *Typographica*, NS no. 13, June 1966. Spread from 'Tombstone lettering on slate' by Frederick Burgess.

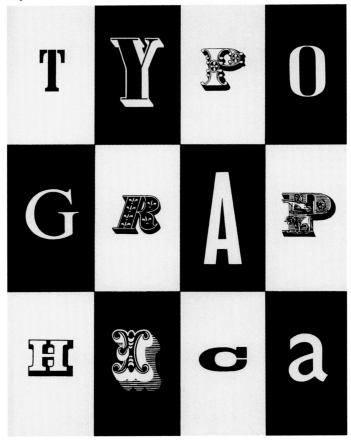

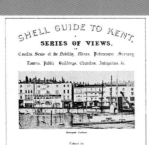

1. This page by John Betjeman was reproduced in the issue of *Typography* shown in 2.

2. A page from the second number of the pioneering journal, *Typography*, edited by Robert Harling (Shenval Press, Spring, 1937).

3. Braque and Picasso were among the first in the twentieth century to recognise the visual attractiveness of nineteenth-century exotics. Here is a later collage, *Eintrittskarte-Merz* 456, done in 1922 by the German artist Kurt Schwitters.

4. *The Architectural Review* began to enliven its pages with 'Egyptians' as early as 1935, and by the time of the second world war was one of the major advocates of the older types – showing their use in architecture as well as in typography. At the same time, the layout of the *Review* became more and more free of old restrictions. In this page (from the September 1954 issue) shaded and grotesque types are used in an unmistakably twentieth-century setting.

Old-fashioned Types and New-fangled Typography

A study in the revival of nineteenth-century exotic type faces, by Alan M. Fern

It is generally agreed, I think, that Emery Walker and William Morris emerged victorious from their battle to reform typography. First the private presses and then the journals – *The Imprint* and *The Fleuron* – disposed of the old taste and instituted their own. First in England and soon after elsewhere in the world shoddy printing, eccentrically and poorly designed, gave way to carefully considered, harmonious typography. A trade was turned into an art. If the typography of the Bauhaus differed from that of the English designers, at least both groups treated letters as the basic and immutable stuff of typography design. As the twentieth century advanced, extraneous ornament disappeared from the page, types were redesigned in terms of carefully enunciated principles, and confirmation for all this was found in history – especially in the first hundred years of printing. The letters must not depart from their proper forms; the tools – whether hand-tools or machine-tools – must be clearly related to the letter-forms which they create. Theories of readability and clarity were on the lips of every advanced typographer.

What has occurred, then, to bring about the revival today of mid-nineteenth-century grotesque and decorated letters – letters which defy justification in terms of the typographic reforms of the past sixty-five years? For Victorian letters are found today widely used in display typography, in advertising, and on buildings. 'Egyptians' and 'fat-faces' have become again a common part of the designer's vocabulary, and new letters have been designed in the spirit of the old (indeed, 'Chisel' is an adaptation of an older 'Latin' which was solid in its earlier form).

Actually the reform of typography was not so extensive as it is generally regarded. Men like Andrew W. Tuer and Will Bradley refused to be talked out of their enthusiasm for the exuberant and even crude nineteenth-century types (and the illustrations which accompanied them) and their work in this vein around the turn of the century was enjoyed by a sizeable audience. Then, too, the provincial printer kept to his old ways. Typefounders never discontinued their time-honoured faces, so while the Chiswick Press and the followers of Morris were preaching the gospel according to Caslon and Jenson the printer in Wales could buy all the 'Bold Latin' or 'Thorowgood Italic' he needed. This was demonstrated graphically to John Piper and J. M. Richards, when they were travelling in Lincolnshire seventeen years ago. As they passed a printer's shop in Louth they were struck with admiration by the samples visible in his window. Hurriedly they composed a broadside – a text celebrating the town's architectural wonders – and entering the shop they ordered a few copies printed as the printer thought best. They repaired to a pub to allow him to work undisturbed, and when they returned found that he had produced a masterpiece of Victorian printing. No less than eleven type faces are used for the twenty-five lines of the page!

So the materials of Victorian typography had not disappeared. Nevertheless, the provincial printer was entirely neglected by the twentieth-century critic of typography, except that perhaps his work was regarded as typical of all that was unenlightened and illegible in printing. Tuer and Bradley were considered

---

Various conceits in continuous line showed the writing-masters' 'command of hand'. Here Wood of Bingham (left) and Bonser of Clipston (below) employ a dove and a swan to carry the superscription.

A few treatments gathered at random of letter 'H'. Rubbings are an easy medium for amassing records of lettering.

John Ayres – the southern work having no sign of calligraphic influence. Early lettering has a directness of approach in scoring anything but the mere scratching-in of line widths as a preliminary to cutting, that often leads to such makeshifts of spacing as we tend to admire today as being honest and uninhibited rather than careless." There is little evidence to support the theory, but it has been suggested that the organized and deliberate design of later inscriptions may have been due to a preliminary painting-in of the letters. It seems fair to assume that elaborate headings with their maze of

"This vernacular tradition might well be given a contemporary application. There would seem an opportunity here for town or country districts to break away from the use of any sterile pantopian letter-forms for the naming of their streets, shops, and public and industrial buildings, and contrive instead an idiomatic sign-language to express regional characteristics.

12

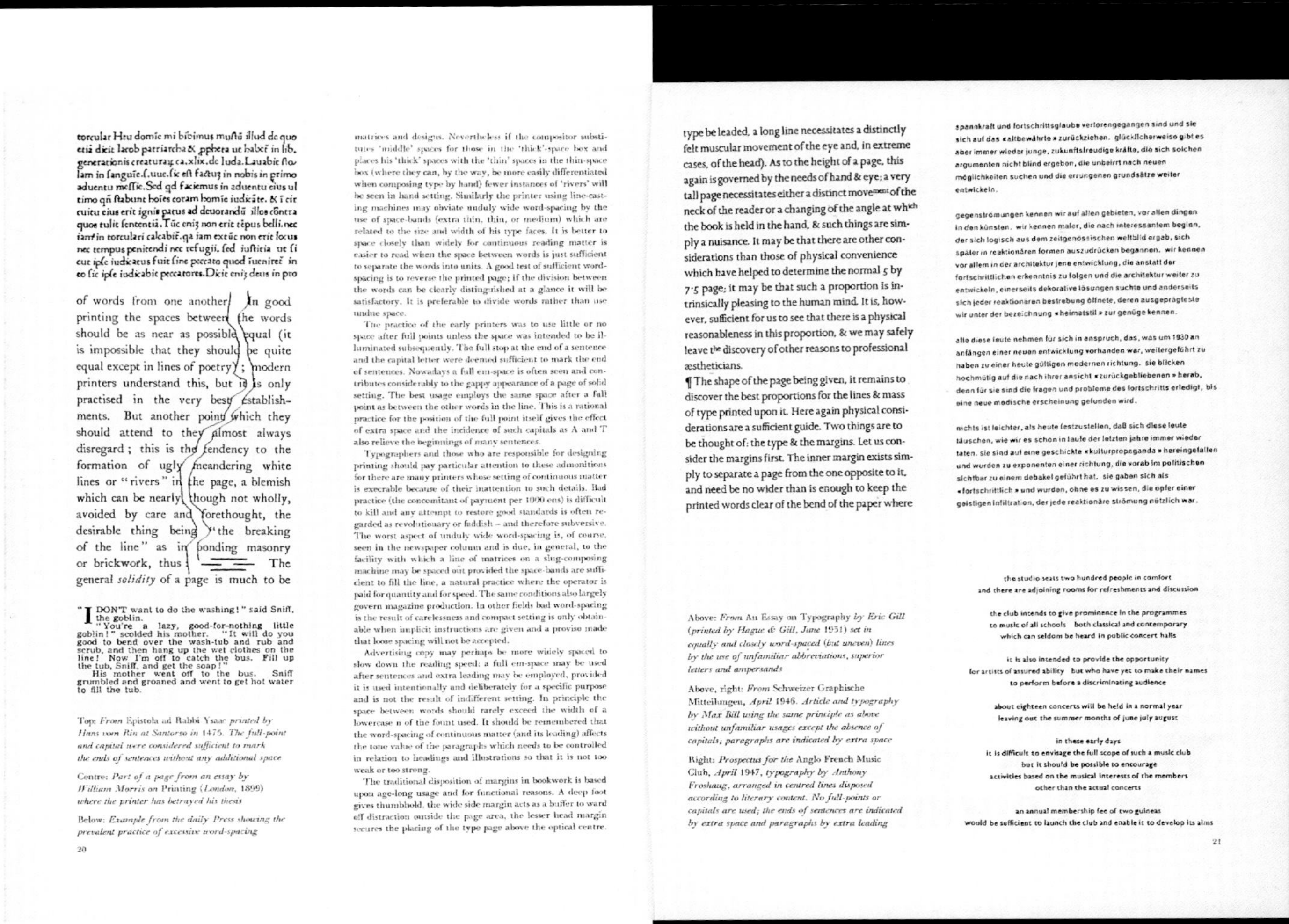

Above: *Typographica*,
OS no. 1, 1949. Spread from
'The use of space in
typography' by John Tarr.
Typography by Max Bill
from *Schweizer Graphische
Mitteilungen*, April 1946,
is shown top right. Anthony
Froshaug's prospectus for
the Anglo French Music
Club, April 1947, is shown
bottom right.
Right: Catalogue cover for
the Kunsthaus Zürich, 1947,
210 × 147 mm. Design: Max
Bill. Reproduced (as line
artwork) in *Typographica*,
OS no. 2, 1950.

Opposite: *Typographica*,
OS no. 2, 1950. Page from
'Typographical review',
showing invitation card
designed by Anthony
Froshaug, 1949 (original
black on green, 105 ×
148 mm).

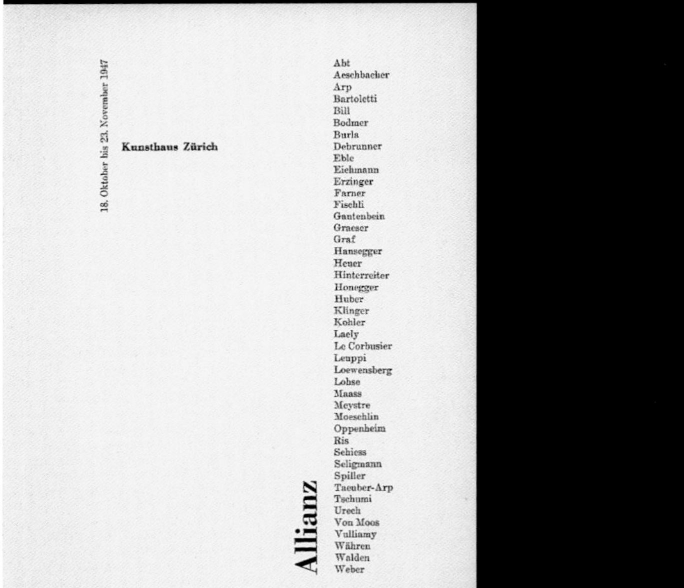

design that Spencer will feel a periodic need to qualify.

Even before the reader encountered Spencer's introductory editorial, the first issue of *Typographica* signalled its modernist intentions with its cover. The magazine's title is placed in an aggressive wing-shaped device held in asymmetrical balance with a large number 1. The colours are constructivist: red, white and black, against a grey background. Inside, an article by John Tarr on the use of space in typography is significant less for its main text than for the 'notes on some typographical experiments' and illustrations that accompany it.[10] Spencer included a page designed by Hans Schleger from *The Practice of Design* (1946), showing 'adroit use of sub-headings', as well as two examples by Bill and a prospectus for the Anglo French Music Club (1947) by Froshaug to demonstrate all-lower case setting, the use of line-spacing to mark paragraph breaks and, in Froshaug's case, the use of extra inter-word spacing, instead of full-points, to indicate the ends of sentences. Bill and Froshaug make an immediate reappearance in a 'Typographical review' in OS no. 2, where an invitation card by Froshaug and a catalogue cover by Bill are reproduced actual size alongside cover designs by Spencer for the Architectural Press and by his colleague Ian Bradbery for the Society of Industrial Artists – an unambiguous gesture of allegiance by Spencer.

Bill and Froshaug were significant contributors, too, to the exhibition 'Purpose and Pleasure' organized in 1952 by Spencer, Anthony Bell of Lund Humphries and *Typographica* contributor

49

TYPOGRAPHICA **Typographical Review**

1 Invitation card, designed and printed by Anthony Froshaug for Rudolf Steiner Hall. Size 4½ ins × 5⅞ ins. Original in black on green board.

2 Cover for S.I.A. Journal, designed by Ian Bradbery. Original printed in blue and black on white.

3 Book catalogue cover, designed by Herbert Spencer for The Architectural Press. Original printed in grey and black on white.

4 Catalogue cover, designed by Max Bill, Zurich. Original printed in black on yellow.

All these designs are here reproduced actual size: Nos. 1 and 4 from line blocks, Nos. 2 and 3 from the original blocks and type.
The size of the card below (the maximum allowed for postcards under international postal regulations) has been made standard by Froshaug for all invitation cards designed by him.

Rudolf Steiner Hall Licensee F W Goodman 33 Park Road London N W 1

Goethe Bicentenary Presentation / 7pm 25 & 26 April 1949

ELEONORE SCHJELDERUP

in her original dramatic rendering in German of Goethe's **Faust**
First appearance in England after successful tour of Western Germany where Press commented : an astonishing achievement . the multitude of characters come to life through El. Schjelderup's great artistry . an arresting personality . in the front rank of German artists

Advance enquiries HAMpstead 36 09
Box Office open 10-1 daily from Monday 18 April PADdington 99 67

1 Set in Gill Medium, Gill Bold, and Minster Black.

25

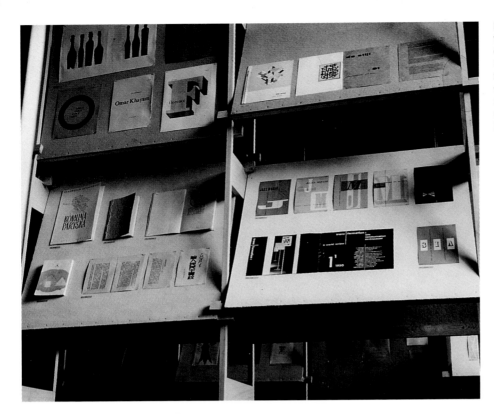

50   Michael Middleton. The international survey of posters, stationery, invitation cards, greetings cards, announcements, exhibition catalogues, trade catalogues, balance sheets, press ads, booklets, books and magazines included work from Britain (Froshaug, Bradbery, Ruari McLean, John Denison-Hunt), the United States (Paul Rand, Herbert Matter, Will Burtin, Erik Nitsche), Switzerland (Tschichold, Bill, Reiner, Max Caflisch, Walter Bosshardt), Italy (Huber), France (Faucheux) and The Netherlands (Sandberg), as well as examples from Sweden, Czechoslovakia, Poland and China. Froshaug was represented by 13 examples, four illustrated in *Typographica*; Bill by 12 examples, four illustrated.[11] The exhibition was perhaps the most concerted statement of public support in Britain, up to that date, for the contemporary typographic style.

Bill was also one of five eminent designers and printers asked to give their views on contemporary trends in typography in the catalogue issue. He argues for the redundancy of the thick rules, dots and excessively large page numbers that had characterized the new typography of the 1930s – 'they are as unnecessary as any other ornament and their omission makes for a simpler and cleaner layout'.[12] By now a fixture in *Typographica*, he reappears in OS no. 6, arguing, perhaps unexpectedly, against the need for standardization of book spines. In OS no. 7, Spencer's fascination with a designer he had first encountered on his post-war travels in 1948 is consummated in Anthony Hill's eight-page profile, the first consideration of the full range of his activities

Typographica No. 5 – a special issue containing over eighty illustrations (many in colour) of post-war printing design – is devoted to

PURPOSE AND

an exhibition

PLEASURE

A review of book, magazine and commercial printing from fourteen countries.
Contributors include Max Bill, Paul Rand, Herbert Simon, James Shand, W. J. H. B. Sandberg

Lund Humphries   5/-

12
Posters

Anthologie
de la POÈSIE
NATURELLE

présenté par
Camille Bryen
& Alain
Gheerbrant

En vente ICI VIENT
de paraître avec
8 photographies
de Brassaï. 390 frs

K editeur.

Pierre Faucheux, *France*

jacob
BENDIEN

stedelijk museum a'dam
7-30 sept. '51

W. J. H. B. Sandberg, *Holland*

13
Posters

ROYAL
FESTIVAL
HALL

Donald Gardner, *England*

BUILDING
GOOD HOUSES

EXHIBITION
OF METHODS OF RESEARCH
IN HOUSE CONSTRUCTION

ADMISSION FREE

Charles Hasler, *England*

Vient de
paraître.
En vente
ICI.

Henri
Pichette: LES
EPIPHANIES
Texte intégral de la
pièce présentée pour
la première fois le 3
Décembre 1947, aux
Noctambules.
K. EDITEUR,

Pierre Faucheux, *France*

congrès international
d'architecture
moderne   22-31 juillet 1949

7
ciam
bergamo   palazzo della ragione

Max Huber, *Italy*

ABOVE AND RIGHT:
W. J. H. B. Sandberg, *Holland*

stedelijk museum a'dam

'T
PAAPJE

bedrukte
en geweven stoffen

9 nov.
9 dec.

la biennale
di venezia

XIV FESTIVAL
INTERNAZIONALE
DI MUSICA
CONTEMPORANEA

FESTIVAL
INTERNAZIONALE
DEL
TEATRO

Italy

16
Book Jackets and Covers

JAZZ MUSIC   VOL 4   NO 4   PRICE 1/6

9
nona triennale
di milano

maggio-settembre 1951

Max Huber, *Italy*

la Rinascente

Max Huber, *Italy*

17
Booklets and Folders

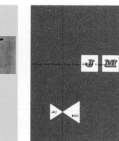

Ian Bradbery, *England*

JAZZ MUSIC

JAZZ MUSIC

Gordon Andrews, *England*

Pierre Faucheux, *France*

SOLEIL
COU
COUPÉ
par Aimé Césaire

K éditeur
Le Quadrangle

JAZZ MUSIC

Albe Steiner, *Italy*

to be published in English. In this special inset, laid out by Bill himself, Spencer allowed Bill to break with *Typographica*'s established, still relatively conservative typographic style in every aspect, even including the style of the folios, and specify all-lower case, full-out, line-spaced paragraphs, and ranged-left setting. This was a bold, if not incendiary, gesture in the European backwater of British typography and, while Spencer was sufficiently committed to experimentation to introduce the possibility of such a layout, in his judgement it would have been impossible to present the entire magazine in this style. In content too, it was the most uncompromising – and no doubt, for many readers, demanding – article published up to this point. The particularities of professional typography are left far behind in an essay that passionately argues the need to reunite art and design and to reintegrate the plastic arts with everyday life. Bill, revealed here fully for the first time as architect, painter, sculptor, industrial designer, typographer, educator and writer, is seen as a figure capable of developing, through his commitment to 'concrete art', the synthesis initiated by earlier experimentalists such as Van Doesburg, Le Corbusier and Moholy-Nagy.

In *Design in Business Printing*, published the same year as 'Purpose and Pleasure', and part of the same reformist drive, Spencer unites a brief account of typographic history, from Artistic Printing to the Bauhaus, with practical advice and instructional examples. Some readers must have been puzzled by the lessons of Futurism, Dada and Apollinaire's calligramme

Above: *Typographica*, OS no. 7, 1953. Page from 'Max Bill' by Anthony Hill. Design: Max Bill.
Left: *Design in Business Printing*, 1952, 246 × 360 mm. Spread showing Futurist design by Ardengo Soffici, 1915. Design: Spencer. Publisher: Sylvan Press.

'THE PRESENT PERIOD IS CRITICAL. IT IS ONE OF APPREHENSION AND SPECULATION, AND ALSO OF AWARENESS THAT DYNAMIC CONCEPTIONS ARE BECOMING STATIC AND STERILE; HOWEVER, THE REMEDY DOES NOT LIE IN FURTHER INNOVATION, OR IN A TOTAL REASSESSMENT, BUT IN THE HARDER TASK OF CONSOLIDATION AND PURPOSEFUL RESEARCH TOWARDS UNITY.'

ANTHONY HILL, 'MAX BILL', 1953

'Il pleut' for restaurant wine lists and Van Heusen shirt advertisements, and Spencer, having assembled these provocative examples, issues a note of caution: 'None of the last three had any lasting influence on the development of display typography but indicated an awareness of the need for new forms of presentation.'[13] Of greatest importance, he notes, was the Bauhaus. Three years later, writing in *Ark* about recent developments in typography, he is even more emphatic in his attempt to establish the limits of contemporary typographic ambition. While the designs of the early pioneers

> . . . were revolutionary in conception and spectacular in effect . . . nothing comparable is happening today. And nothing as spectacular should be expected. The task facing the creative worker today is not the discovery of new continents but rather the exploration and full exploitation of what has recently been discovered.[14]

Spencer nevertheless remained fascinated by the new typographic continents discovered by the early modernists. The sixth issue includes a three-page note on the Dutch designer Piet Zwart, which is used as an opportunity to take contemporary typography to task for its lack of vigour. Spencer wrote another short article, on the Dutch printer-painter H. N. Werkman, for OS no. 11. Not until OS no. 16, however, did he begin in earnest his reappraisal of the origins of the new typography by publishing a detailed profile of El Lissitzky by Camilla Gray, daughter of Nicolete Gray and author, in 1962, of the ground-breaking study *The Great Experiment: Russian Art 1863–1922*. Gray's article ends

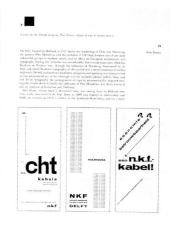

Above: *Typographica*, OS no. 6, 1952. Spread from 'Piet Zwart', a brief, unsigned note, by Spencer. Below: *Typographica*, NS no. 7, May 1963, Spread from 'Piet Zwart' by Spencer.

53

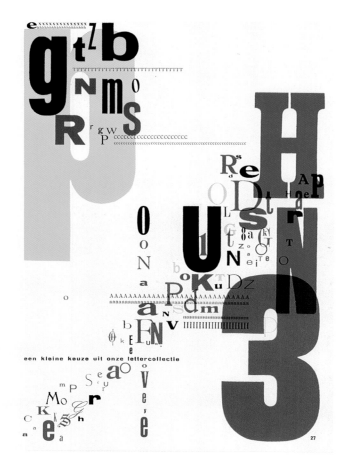

Van Doesburg, the Bauhaus was dominated by de Stijl during its early years until the effect of the constructivist congress held in Weimar in 1922 and, more specifically, the appointment to the teaching staff of the Hungarian Moholy-Nagy later the same year, modified its direction. But although Moholy-Nagy was able to develop Russian Constructivism as a powerful pedagogic method, de Stijl continued to exert a considerable influence both on the Bauhaus and on the whole subsequent course of European typography, design, and architecture.

Piet Zwart made his first contact with de Stijl in 1919 and from then until 1921 he worked as assistant to Jan Wils, a member of the Stijl group. About this time, too, he began teaching evening classes at the Academie Rotterdam, an activity he continued until 1932; Dick Elffers was one of his pupils there. In 1921 Zwart became assistant to the famous Dutch architect H. P. Berlage; the Christian Science church in The Hague is one of the buildings which Zwart worked on with Berlage during the next four years. It was while working in Berlage's office that Zwart produced his first typographical designs – for Vickers House in The Hague – and carried out

Page from a printer's catalogue (Trio, The Hague) designed by Piet Zwart in 1929, opposite, and an advertisement for Nederlandsche Kabelfabriek, 1928, below

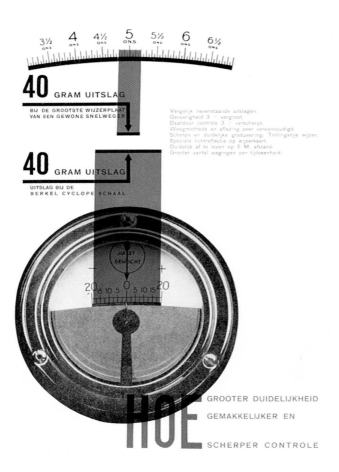

of pictorial expression were accepted everywhere. The camera took the place of the brush in the hands of the artist to depict documentary sketches and human documents. It was a quicker, simpler, more direct and more varied method of expression.'

Again, as with still photography, Schuitema had to teach himself. Partly for economic reasons (but also because he was impatient to know what he had achieved) he developed and printed the films himself. His use of fine grain developer produced a broad tonal scale and enabled him to make good paper prints from the film negatives. But, on the other hand, his dense negatives gave much trouble to the laboratory that had later to make his final film copies.

Between 1929 and 1939 Schuitema made three films: *De Bruggen* (the bridges of Rotterdam), *De hallen* (the Paris food market, Les Halles) and *De Bouwhoek* (a country district in the province of Friesland in the north of Holland). Although he did not start working on all three at once they were in fact simultaneously conceived as related explorations of movement. *De Bruggen* is concerned primarily with the movement of things; *De hallen* with the movement of people. In the third film, *De Bouwhoek*, it is the camera that moves over an unmoving land.

After the second world war Schuitema made several further films, including *The Partisan's Song*, an experiment in the movement of colour. But since the death in 1953 of his close friend, Koos van der Griend (who composed the sound for *De Bruggen* and Schuitema's post-war films), Schuitema has made no further films.

A brochure and a press advertisement designed by Paul Schuitema for Berkel.

41

54   ***Typographica***, NS no. 8,
December 1963. Spread
from 'Paul Schuitema'
by Benno Wissing.

with a re-statement of Lissitzky's eight prophetic typographic principles.[15] In 1963, Spencer returned to Zwart, on the occasion of an exhibition at Lund Humphries, his first public showing in Britain.[16] Articles by other writers followed, throughout the new series, on the innovations of Paul Schuitema, Henryk Berlewi and other Polish designers, Alexander Rodchenko and Kurt Schwitters. Although Spencer had announced his intention, in his introduction to *Typographica*'s first issue, to comment upon 'typographical experiments of significance' he had made no specific reference to historical experiments. In his final editorial, in *Typographica*, NS no. 16, with the achievement of 32 issues to reflect on, he explains his intentions. Among other aims, he wanted:

> . . . to try to set in perspective the experimental work of the first half of this century and to record and evaluate the work of those pioneers of the 'twenties and early 'thirties who helped to establish a new aesthetic and to formulate the vocabulary of today's designers.[17]

Spencer's *Typographica* texts on Zwart and Werkman became the basis for the sections on these designers in *Pioneers of Modern Typography*.[18] All of the new typographers featured over the years in *Typographica* are revisited, and many of the same examples are included, making the book an extension of the *Typographica* project.[19] The tension between the spectacular experiments of the past – which often proceed from a revolutionary impulse – and the use that today's 'creative worker' is supposed to make of them is not, however, something that *Pioneers* can resolve.

The effect of concentrating so many examples between its covers only serves to emphasize the divide. After the explosive provocations of the Futurist and Dadaist typography shown in the book's introduction, Spencer's conclusion strikes a reductively pragmatic note, as work created in highly specific cultural and political contexts is held up as source of the most generalized professional lesson:

> The fundamental difference between traditional, centred typography and modern typography is that the one is passive and the other is active, though not necessarily aggressive. Asymmetry and contrast provide the basis of modern typography . . .
>
> The debates about typefaces, about serifs, and other typographical minutiae which, during the late 'twenties and subsequently, have often surrounded modern typography, have sometimes obscured its fundamental characteristics and the advantages, in terms of visual fluency and clarity, which flow from the imaginative use of contrast and asymmetry.[20]

The pioneers, Spencer concludes, using similar words to those in his final editorial in *Typographica*, have created 'a new and richer visual vocabulary'.

That design history needs to discover a new and richer *critical* vocabulary to discuss the nature and implications of the pioneers' achievement has become increasingly apparent in recent years. The work of the modernist artist-typographers is receiving particular scrutiny. Gérard Mermoz suggests that standard design narratives of Futurism, while acknowledging its historical significance, 'fail to provide an adequate account of futurist typography and an assessment of its contemporary relevance'.[21] Analysis runs aground at the level of unambitious formal description, while the linguistic and poetic content of typographic experiments by a writer such as F. T. Marinetti is overlooked, and even the manifestos which spell out the Futurists' intentions sometimes go unconsulted.[22]

As Spencer points out at the start of *Pioneers*, by the end of the 1920s the 'heroic' period of modern typography initiated by Marinetti and the Futurists was over and the new typography 'had entered a new and different phase, one of consolidation rather than of exploration and innovation'.[23] This phase continued throughout *Typographica*'s first decade and into the 1960s. An alternative reading might see the process of consolidation by which typographic art was reconciled to the professional exigencies of the 'Art of Typography' – Spencer's phrase – less in terms of what was gained (a new 'vocabulary') than in terms of what was lost (a truly experimental typographic avant-garde). This is the view taken by Johanna Drucker in her conclusion to *The Visible Word*, an examination of experimental typography as a modern art practice.

Drucker focuses on four poets active in typographic experimentation in the 1910s and 1920s: Marinetti, Apollinaire, Ilia Zdanevich and the Dadaist Tristan Tzara. Her concern is the 'materiality' of this work, which she defines as 'the self-conscious attention to the formal means of production in literature and

55

Typographica, NS no. 9, June 1964. Opening spread from 'Henryk Berlewi and Mechano-faktura' by Eckhard Neumann.

the visual arts'.[24] She argues that in the work of a designer such as Zwart, who did not begin to produce typographic designs until the mid-1920s, the 'visual codes of earlier avant-garde activity became subsumed under the well-ordered behaviors of advertising display'.[25] Not until the arrival of concrete poetry, in the post-war period, she suggests, were these codes returned to literary practice. These avant-garde experiments, undertaken outside the restrictive fields of corporate communications and advertising, were of the greatest interest to Spencer. From the late 1950s, he published articles about them in *Typographica* while simultaneously revisiting the historical origins of modern typography.

In *Typographica*'s first decade, the consolidation of the lessons of the typographic pioneers into a reformed commercial practice was encouraged in two ways. First, Spencer published occasional articles on typographic practice and reform. His own 'Function & design in business printing' was followed, in the first series, by a plea for rational typeface terminology; arguments for and against the standardization of book spines; a discussion of the urgent need to improve the training of typographers; and a bizarre proposal by a Dutch professor to maximize the use of the printed page by employing a multiple-print system, involving the overprinting of green and red capitals that required special glasses to be read. The argument for reform was most convincingly made, however, by visual example. In the 'Purpose and Pleasure' issue, Charles Hasler's 'Building Good Houses'

Below: *Typographica*, OS no. 9, 1954. Spread from 'Recent typography in France' by Edward Wright, showing an example by Pierre Faucheux, bottom left. Opposite: *Typographica*, OS no. 13, 1957. Spread from 'French book clubs' by Germano Facetti, showing opening pages of typical books.

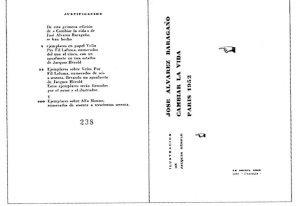

railway stations, in all-over zebra pattern on delivery vans, and on the *pissoirs* in the streets of Paris. He has also designed a colour film and a series of illuminated signs for the same product. All his work retains the typical Swiss virtues of delicacy and precision.

Hofer, who is a printer and also Swiss, sometimes works with Hächler, but he is young enough to be rather more influenced by his environment. He admits that in Paris he has developed a more daring colour sense, and the freedom to experiment and the appreciation of the results which he has achieved have both stimulated and rewarded him. Hofer does not pretend to be a designer, but his inspired jobbing printer's approach is accompanied by a strong sense of design and style.

Broadly, the most hopeful characteristics of recent typography in France are a tendency to avoid the 'compass and ruler' types (such as Futura), preferred by modern designers in the 'thirties, in favour of the more human jobbing and newspaper faces of the nineteenth century and the frequent use of large type as a graphic and evocative element.

poster, based on Victorian display types, traditionally centred, looks hopelessly bookish and is entirely overpowered by the articulate, asymmetrical typography of Faucheux and Sandberg that surrounds it. In subsequent issues, Spencer interspersed the few home-grown examples he could find with strong European work: gallery invitations by John Denison-Hunt; recent French typography (much of it, again, by Faucheux); Sandberg's Stedelijk Museum catalogues; Contemporary Art Society invitation cards by Ian Bradbery; Swissair's trilingual print programme; and books published by the French book clubs and by the Büchergilde Gutenberg, a guild of German-speaking printers.

For those with a commitment to change, progress was slow. Ken Garland, writing in 1960, expressed exasperation at those who continued to claim that native English genius could best be expressed in historical forms, and railed at the quantity of published opinion in support of this view. For Garland, there was an urgent need to unite the exuberance of mid-century American graphic design with the orderliness of the new typography as practised by the Swiss to create a new design 'perhaps more serviceable than either' that would be properly sensitive to structure and substance. He ends his reappraisal of the modernists' disregarded design legacy with an anguished *cri de cœur*: 'Was the revolution of the 20's in vain?'[26]

A highly perceptive North American perspective on the enduring post-war problems of British typography was offered, in 1961, by the Canadian designer Allan Fleming, then working

'A LANGUAGE OF VISION HAS BEEN DEFINED . . . IT OFFERS THE MOST EXCITING POSSIBILITIES, BUT IT CANNOT BE SAID TO HAVE SUCCEEDED UNTIL IT HAS PERMEATED EVERY LEVEL OF SOCIETY, BUSINESS, INDUSTRY, POLITICS, ENTERTAINMENT – THE LOT. WE MUST TURN A BLUEPRINT INTO A FUNCTIONING PRODUCT.'

KEN GARLAND, 'STRUCTURE AND SUBSTANCE', 1960

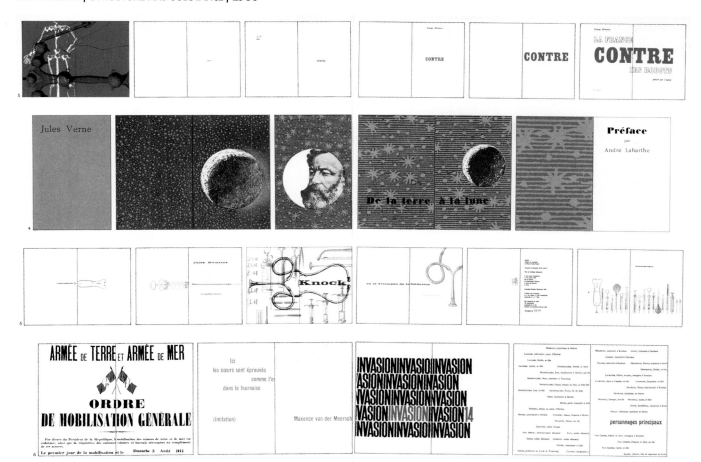

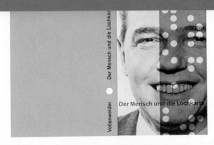

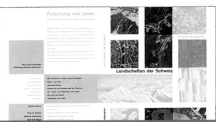

Five wrappers from books published by Büchergilde Gutenberg, Zurich.
The original of *Das Gesetz der Ordnung* is in black only. The other four wrappers are all in two colours (but the colours here have been modified in reproduction).

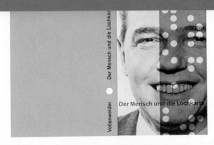

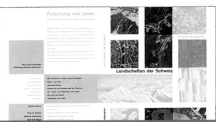

58

in London. Fleming, like Spencer, identifies the dominance of the book tradition in British typography and its inadequacy for the design of printed ephemera and, again like Spencer, singles out Harling's *Typography* as a beacon of pre-war possibility. In Fleming's analysis, the Festival of Britain, and the revival of Victoriana it both encouraged and sanctioned, was a 'disaster'. Spencer's *Design in Business Printing*, on the other hand, was 'the first honest British step, and a long one at that, toward a modern and individual approach to ephemeral design' – except that its followers mistakenly took from it only the narrowest of stylistic pointers.[27]

Fleming argues that the only exceptions to come from an otherwise 'timid' design community are Edward Wright's work, the new designer of *Queen* magazine (Mark Boxer) and Spencer's *Typographica*.[28] As a retrospective diagnosis, Fleming's article is hard to fault, but he does overlook what can be seen with hindsight as the emergence, in the early 1960s, of a new energy and determination among younger designers to forge real change. Fleming, like Garland, points to the vulgar vitality of American design and its lessons for Britain. Others were also looking (or travelling) across the Atlantic,[29] as well as to Switzerland, where the magazine *Neue Grafik* had been started in September 1958 by Richard Lohse, Josef Müller-Brockmann, Hans Neuburg and Carlo Vivarelli. Spencer's ideas had taken firmer hold than Fleming could know. Designers who had studied with Froshaug and Spencer, and pored over *Typographica*, taking its news, discoveries and teachings to heart, would soon bring vigour and vision to the creation of a genuinely contemporary British graphic design. Spencer, as a 'pioneer' in his own right of British new typography, would inevitably be less central, as others took the baton and the focus of preoccupation shifted, in the early 1960s, from the *typographic* to the *graphic*. His magazine would go on, however, in its more liberated second series, to become ever more suggestive in its editorial content, documentary method, juxtapositions and design.

Opposite top: *Typographica*, OS no. 15, 1958. Spread from 'Büchergilde Gutenberg' by Walter Plata, showing five wrappers from books published by the Zurich-based book club. Opposite bottom: *Typographica*, OS no. 11, 1955. Spread from 'Swissair', a note on the printing of the Swiss airline.

Below: *Neue Grafik*, no. 1, September 1958, 278 × 249 mm. Publisher: Verlag Otto Walter AG.

59

'FOR THE NEW TYPE OF BOOK A NEW KIND OF AUTHOR IS EMERGING . . . HE STANDS IN THE SAME RELATION TO THE BOOK AS THE PRODUCER TO THE FILM – GUIDING AND INSPIRING DESIGNERS, TYPOGRAPHERS, ILLUSTRATORS, VISUAL RESEARCH WORKERS AND OTHER EXPERTS BUT IMPOSING UPON ALL HIS OWN CENTRAL CONCEPTION OF HIS THEME.'
HERBERT SPENCER, 'THE FUTURE OF BOOK PRODUCTION', 1963

Typographica 11

4.

The camera as pen

Typographica, NS no. 11, June 1965. Design: Spencer, using a photograph by Magdeleine Blot. (Slightly larger than original.)

Photography was central to *Typographica*'s second series in a way, and to a degree, that has never been adequately recognized in published discussion of the magazine. The difference is immediately apparent on opening the later issues: they contain many more photographs. Photography allowed *Typographica* to leave the controlled conditions of the studio and break free from the confining flatness of line illustration, printed type and the supplied graphic image. In the 1960s, the magazine retained its concern with the letterform as an agent of communication, but a large part of its attention relocated to the street. As in its attitude to typographic experimentation, *Typographica* embodied two apparently contradictory drives. It undertook a documentary audit of the visual landscape and campaigned for its reform by the systematic attentions of the designer. Yet, in the same breath, it celebrated imperfection, random pattern and the ravages of chance. ≫→

From 1959 to 1967, photography was an obsessive interest for Spencer:

> . . . photography is probably one of the most important elements of my life. Although it lasted only for a few years in that form I was very, very committed. And looking back, it's the photographs that give me probably the most pleasure – the greatest sense of achievement . . .[1]

With the camera, Spencer seemed to delight in unravelling the order he spent his days as a designer attempting to impose. His most telling and memorable images, those that seem most fully his own, show a world in which things fall apart, signs of official communication fray into unpredictable poetry, and ordinary people assert their presence and mark their passage by defiantly inscribing streets, buildings and land with messages and marks. He brought a designer's fascination to the exact physical aspect of the objects that caught his attention and he rendered them with a sharp graphic eye. The images that most fully absorbed him were often far removed from the territory or influence of the metropolitan design consultant.

Spencer acquired a Voigtlander Brilliant camera (like a simpler version of the Rolleiflex twin-lens reflex) just after the Second World War and was a careful photographer without, at that stage, becoming engrossed. In the summer of 1959, a national printing strike meant that it was impossible to get anything produced, so Spencer and his family travelled to Rotterdam, The Netherlands, to stay in the apartment of his friend Benno Wissing until the strike was over. In Rotterdam,

Spencer bought a Rolleiflex – not easily available in Britain at that point – and spent a month taking photographs in the docks. In a prophetic early picture from this series, discarded boxes, broken crates and other chunks of driftwood wash up on the pebble-covered isthmus between the man-made sea wall and the uncontrollable sea.

In 1960, Spencer bought a Pentax 35 mm camera and had a darkroom installed in his Blomfield Road house in London, where he would spend the evenings developing and printing his pictures. Seeking to increase his understanding of darkroom techniques, Spencer asked Alfred Lammer, a photography tutor at the Central School and staff photographer of *Design*, to give him weekly lessons.[2] In 1961, Spencer spent two weeks in Italy and took many photographs. The same year, he collaborated with the literary agent Helga Greene on a series of travel guides, with himself as general editor. He spent several weeks in Crete with his family and Greene, taking black and white photographs for the first of the compact 'Albatross' guides. In his design for the book, the pictures are gathered together at the front, in advance of the text, to form a continuous 24-page sequence.[3] Spencer's commitments to *Typographica*, *The Penrose Annual* and his own design practice meant that he was not able to sustain this level of involvement, though he did commission other books in the series. In 1962, he made two long photographic trips – one to Sicily and one to Ireland to take pictures to accompany Heinrich Böll's *Irish Diary* (the English publisher, Putnam, changed its

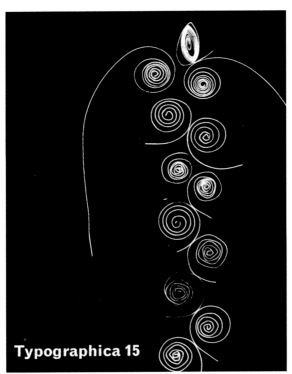

Above: *Typographica*, OS no. 13, 1957. Opening spread from 'The arrow in the road' by Edward Wright. Photographs: Don Hunstein.
Left: *Typographica*, OS no. 15, 1958. Design: Spencer, using photograms by Brian Foster.

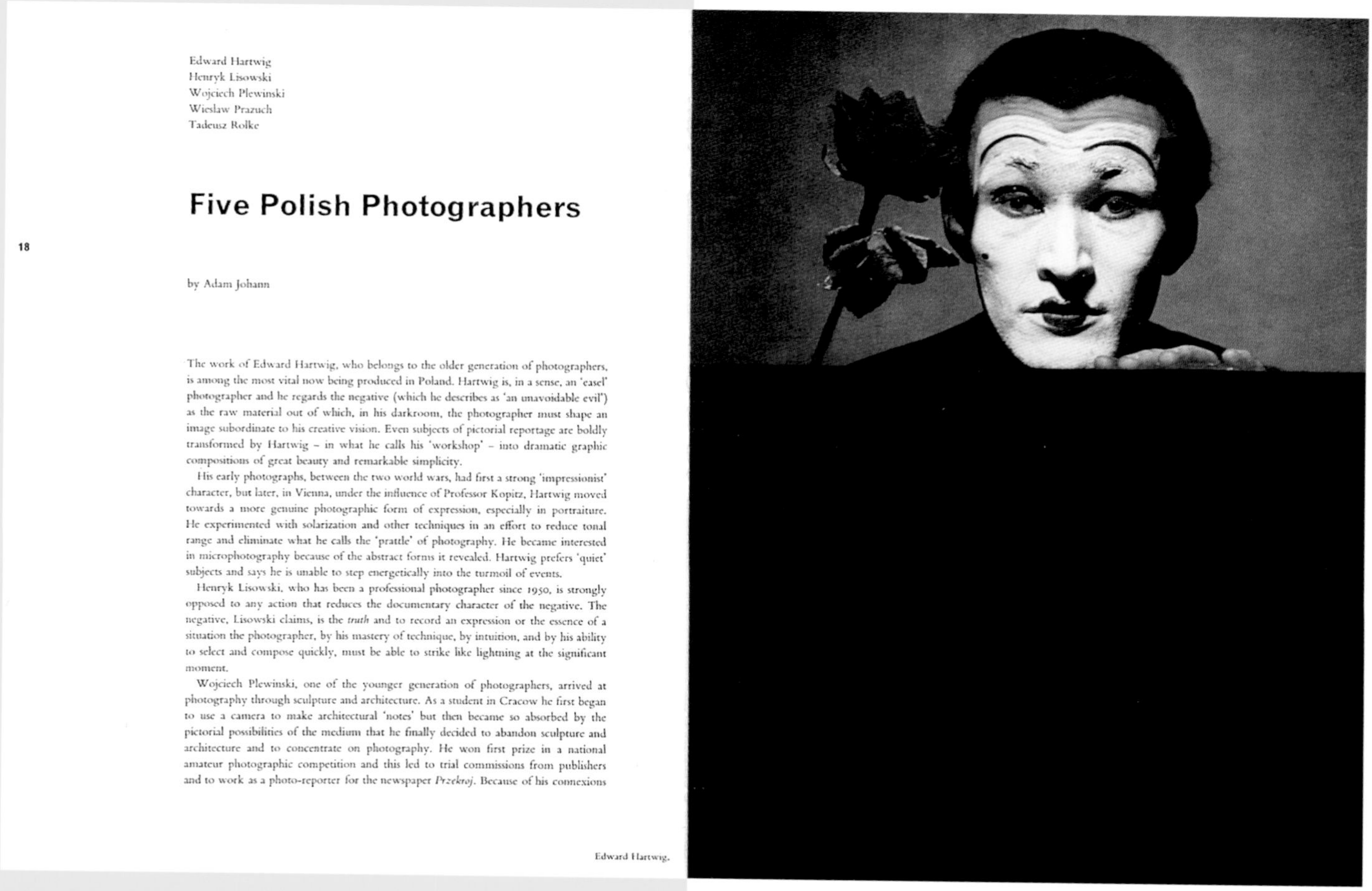

Edward Hartwig
Henryk Lisowski
Wojciech Plewinski
Wieslaw Prazuch
Tadeusz Rolke

Five Polish Photographers

18

by Adam Johann

The work of Edward Hartwig, who belongs to the older generation of photographers, is among the most vital now being produced in Poland. Hartwig is, in a sense, an 'easel' photographer and he regards the negative (which he describes as 'an unavoidable evil') as the raw material out of which, in his darkroom, the photographer must shape an image subordinate to his creative vision. Even subjects of pictorial reportage are boldly transformed by Hartwig – in what he calls his 'workshop' – into dramatic graphic compositions of great beauty and remarkable simplicity.

His early photographs, between the two world wars, had first a strong 'impressionist' character, but later, in Vienna, under the influence of Professor Kopitz, Hartwig moved towards a more genuine photographic form of expression, especially in portraiture. He experimented with solarization and other techniques in an effort to reduce tonal range and eliminate what he calls the 'prattle' of photography. He became interested in microphotography because of the abstract forms it revealed. Hartwig prefers 'quiet' subjects and says he is unable to step energetically into the turmoil of events.

Henryk Lisowski, who has been a professional photographer since 1950, is strongly opposed to any action that reduces the documentary character of the negative. The negative, Lisowski claims, is the *truth* and to record an expression or the essence of a situation the photographer, by his mastery of technique, by intuition, and by his ability to select and compose quickly, must be able to strike like lightning at the significant moment.

Wojciech Plewinski, one of the younger generation of photographers, arrived at photography through sculpture and architecture. As a student in Cracow he first began to use a camera to make architectural 'notes' but then became so absorbed by the pictorial possibilities of the medium that he finally decided to abandon sculpture and architecture and to concentrate on photography. He won first prize in a national amateur photographic competition and this led to trial commissions from publishers and to work as a photo-reporter for the newspaper *Przekroj*. Because of his connexions

Edward Hartwig.

Above: *Typographica*, NS no. 1, June 1960. Opening spread from 'Five Polish photographers' by Adam Johann. Photograph: Edward Hartwig.
Left: *Typographica*, NS no. 2, December 1960. Design: Spencer, based on his photograph of a tree trunk, with carved graffiti, shown in the issue.

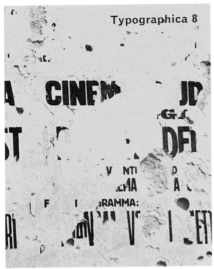

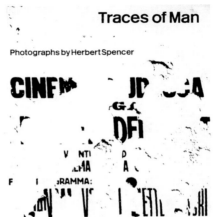

mind so the pictures did not appear). Spencer continued to spend long evenings in the darkroom until 1967, when his many other projects meant he could no longer put so much time into photography. That year, some of the pictures taken on his trips were published by Lund Humphries in the collection *Traces of Man*.[4]

Spencer was influenced by Bill Brandt's lighting and his use of controlled overprinting to form powerful graphic contrasts of black and white. With Lammer's guidance, he preferred Agfa paper and developers that would give rich burnished blacks, while bringing out the detail in the dark areas of a picture. In the photograph of Matt Talbot's shrine in Dublin (1962), the white elements, including the cross and name plate, float with chalky luminescence out of the blackness of the surrounding brickwork. Pictures were carefully composed in the camera so that little if any cropping was required. Cropping was more likely in the case of square-format Rolleiflex pictures, but he tended to use the lighter Pentax for most of his work.

From his earliest pictures in Rotterdam, and again taking photographs in Crete, Spencer found himself drawn ever closer to his subjects until the details that interested him were sometimes just a few feet away. 'It wasn't a conscious plan, but I found the things which were significant for me were the close-ups of details and particularly what, afterwards, I regarded as chance art.'[5] As he proceeded, he discovered, again without any conscious intention, that most of his photographs – certainly those that meant most to him – were devoid of people, though not without a human 'presence'.

Spencer's subject became the gradual accretions and processes of attrition that slowly coalesce to form graphic pattern: names scratched into a park bench[6]; a huge metal street arrow pointing towards scattered blocks of stone; walls treated as unofficial blackboards 'upon which to protest, proclaim, and attempt to persuade'[7]; tattered posters layered on other posters so that random word fragments fuse to suggest new meanings; half-demolished houses in which tiles, fireplaces, wall decorations, floor sections and landings are exposed for speculative reconstruction by the viewer – like the findings of an archaeology of the present. In one of his most complex

Top: *Typographica*, NS no. 8, December 1963. Design and photograph: Spencer. Centre: *Traces of Man* by Spencer, 1967, 233 × 261 mm. Design: Spencer. Publisher: Lund Humphries. Left: Spencer photographing a cave near Mondello, Sicily, 1962.

64

Matt Talbot's shrine,
Dublin, 1962,
by Spencer.

66

Bar Toto, Rome, 1961,
by Spencer.

68

Above: Wall with graffiti,
Rotterdam, c.1962, by
Spencer, published in
Typographica, NS no. 8.
Right: Alternative view,
with Spencer's daughter,
Mafalda.

Wall with graffiti, Noto,
Sicily, 1962, by Spencer,
published in *Typographica*,
NS no. 8.

Typographica, NS no. 8, December 1963. Spreads from 'Chance' by Barbara Jones, with 17 photographs by Spencer.

Poster sites in Monreale, Sicily, and signboards at Hammersmith, London.

Roof of a barn, Ireland, and tobacco kiosk under snow, Switzerland.

70

and original compositions, seen in Rome in 1961, the street wall of the Bar Toto becomes both palimpsest and collage, as successive modes of communication overlay but never entirely obliterate earlier styles of graphic address: stone-carved lettering, graffiti, post box, advertising, neon sign. Missing nothing, the typographer's eye fits the stray 'D' of a sign in a nearby doorway into the visual text.

In *Typographica*, NS no. 8, Spencer published 17 of his photographs accompanied by a short essay written in response to them at Spencer's suggestion by Barbara Jones after they had looked through the pictures together. 'Decay', suggests Jones, 'is the most powerful medium for the improvement of cities… decay, not the architect, adds the last touches, blackens and peels

the stone, applies lichens and cracks, softens the edges, elaborates elaboration…' And the hand of man, she continues, 'works even better than the forces of nature towards the production of chance art, so successfully sometimes that the higher flights of graffiti are works of art with no chance about them'.[8] For the photographer, the task was to discover and isolate these spontaneously formed but easily overlooked expressions of 'chance art'. In *Traces of Man*, Spencer writes:

These photographs, taken over a period of several years and in many countries, have one characteristic in common: pattern. But it is pattern of a special kind for in taking them my aim has been to capture not formal pattern but *expressive* pattern … Occasionally, some detail in the landscape, some fragment of a wall, some echo of the cut and thrust of man and nature, seems to assert itself and vibrate with more significance than the rest.[9]

Spencer's phase as a photographer was short-lived and, despite his commitment, it was never his primary activity.[10] As an article in the *British Journal of Photography* noted, he belonged to an elusive new category, neither professional nor amateur, but dedicated to using the camera as a recorder of 'acute visual situations'.[11] Given his starting point within design practice, Spencer is most appropriately positioned in relation to the tradition of British architectural photography exemplified by Eric de Maré, a regular contributor to *The Architectural Review* and many other publications.[12] The photographer, writes de Maré, can 'discover and reveal architecture where none was intended by creating abstract compositions of an architectonic quality – perhaps from a ruined wall, an old motor car, or a pile of box lids'.[13] Making due allowances for their different choices of subject matter and detail, this abstract 'architectonic' approach to composition has much in common with Spencer, whose pictures would not look out of place beside de Maré's. His fascination with the 'decay' wrought by human hands is the dark side of de Maré's clean and muscular vision of the power and durability of man-made structures. Reflecting on his own practice, and examining the photographs of his colleagues, Spencer came to the conclusion

> . . . that there was a big difference between the approach of a designer or architect and that of the professional photographer. By virtue of one's training or experience one simply looked at things in a different way and selected details and viewpoints which the professional photographer wouldn't have chosen.[14]

In *Typographica*, NS no. 9, Spencer followed up his 'Chance' collection by publishing a portfolio of 27 photographs by designers, painters and architects, among them Peter Chamberlin, Geoffry Powell, Alan Irvine, Michael Middleton, Alan Bartram, Alan Fletcher and himself, as well as pictures by the English surrealists Paul Nash and Humphrey Spender. In the accompanying essay – given the title 'Sunday photographers' – Michael Middleton argues that the camera has become almost as basic a means of communication as writing:

> . . . it is among those trained to evaluate visual criteria as part of some professional discipline – the visually sophisticated but commercially uncommitted – that the most exciting photography is done. Architects and designers pre–eminently, it seems . . . have collectively brought into being a considerable corpus of exciting material, tucked away normally in cupboards and files and never seen outside the immediate circle.[15]

By the time these remarks were published, in 1964, photography was as basic to the editorial conception and structure of *Typographica* as writing, a graphic demonstration, through purposeful design, of Moholy-Nagy's assertion that photography was the medium of a new kind of literacy. The conventional editorial hierarchy, with its routine, unquestioned subordination of image to word, was reversed. In the first series, the illustrations, whether photographic or otherwise, tend in

Typographica, NS no. 9, June 1964. Spread from 'Sunday photographers' by Michael Middleton. Photographs: Spencer, left; Middleton, top right; Alan Fletcher, bottom right.

71

quantity and arrangement to support the text. In the second series, the amount of page space devoted to photographic imagery within articles such as Jones's and Middleton's massively outweighs the space allotted to the writing. Both articles were written in response to collections of images rather than the images being selected to demonstrate and reinforce points in the text. Spencer, too, was approaching the editing process in a different way:

> I suppose because I was involved in photography I saw editorial subjects all around me which could only be realised through photography. Things like issue no. 4 – that couldn't have been done any other way . . . I always had a camera with me at that period so one could immediately, as it were, write the article.[16]

One of the most intensive and spectacular demonstrations of this approach is *Typographica*, NS no. 4, published in December 1961. The issue consists of four long articles, each one concerned with signs and lettering in the street. Two hundred and eight photographs, taken specially for the magazine, are packed into just 72 editorial pages. They represent the full span of Spencer's environmental interests – reformist and *laissez faire* – from his own campaigning feat of roadside documentation in 'Mile-a-minute typography?', to the pleasures of 'primitive street "typography" and the accidents of juxtaposition' discovered by Robert Brownjohn (1925–70) during a weekend spent pounding the London pavements, camera at the ready.[17]

In July 1961, Spencer, driven by his assistant Brian Little,

undertook the 20-mile journey from Marble Arch in central London to London Airport (now Heathrow), stopping as they went to photograph the road signs seen *en route*. They revealed an 'extraordinary barrage of prose',

> . . . a jumbled jungle of words in a vast range of styles, on panels of many different shapes, sizes and colours, mounted on walls, on lamp standards, and on wood, metal, and concrete supports of many kinds, and varying in height from twenty feet, or more, down to within a few inches of the ground – and, indeed, sometimes actually resting on the ground propped up with old cans or rubble.[18]

Spencer laid out most of his 51 photographs as a continuous, eight-page sequence of black and white pictures of varying shapes and sizes, with no text other than the briefest of descriptive captions ('Park Lane improvements', 'The road to London Airport'). Few of the pictures have much aesthetic quality in themselves (compared to, say, his *Traces of Man* work): this would distract from their campaigning purpose.[19] 'Mile-a-minute typography?' was a highly effective polemical contribution to a discussion about British road signs that had been under way since the mid-1950s and would not be resolved until the introduction, in 1964, of Jock Kinneir's modular sign system for all British roads.[20] Spencer's report drew responses in editorials in *The Guardian* and *The Times Literary Supplement*.[21]

Typographica, NS no. 4's two other features, a report on the Civic Trust and lettering in Epping by Nicolete Gray (with photographs by Spencer) and Robert Brownjohn's 'Street level', also make use of

Below: *Typographica*, NS no. 4, December 1961. Spreads from 'Mile-a-minute typography?' Text and photographs: Spencer.

Bond Street, London
Photo Herbert Spencer

◀ Rome – near the Spanish Steps
Photo Herbert Spencer

45

Left and below left: *Signs in Action* by James Sutton, 1965, 197 × 328 mm. Spreads with photographs by Spencer. Publisher: Studio Vista.

Overleaf
Top left: *Typographica*, NS no. 9, June 1964. Spread from 'Crowns' by Camilla Gray, with 13 photographs by Spencer.
Bottom left: *Typographica*, NS no. 12, December 1965. Spread from 'The living symbol'. Text and photographs: Aloisio Magalhães.
Top right: *Typographica*, NS no. 13, June 1966. Opening spread from 'Hong Kong signs'. Text and photographs: Henry Steiner.
Bottom right: *Typographica*, NS no. 12, December 1965. Spread from 'Fishing figures' by Barbara Jones, with 16 photographs by Spencer.

Arrows in a brick road, Amsterdam
Photo Herbert Spencer

Corrugated sign, Park Lane, London
Photo Herbert Spencer

This rough and ready arrow is surprisingly subtle and effective. The ripple of the corrugated iron and the curves of the arrow-head give the message life, urgency and elegance.

A road of arrows.

Garage sign, West London
Photo Herbert Spencer

This shy little notice hopes it will not attract too much attention. It is outside a filling station on a busy road. It would be more at home pointing to fresh eggs and cut flowers in a country lane.

20

21

73

Park Lane improvements

The road to London Airport

7

8

9

A Greek ornamental crown which
reflects the Byzantine closed cap-like
form of crown in contrast to the
Western European open forms built
up of sharp upward-thrusting points

Left and below:
Fairground stalls at Hampstead Heath
(the upper one shows
a form of low arched crown
which came in with
Elizabeth 1; the lower
is the modern shape
worn by Elizabeth II)

Right:
Topping the gate at Holland Park,
Kensington, and again in more stylized
form surmounting the monogram, is an
English baron's coronet.
As worn this would be a golden circlet
encrusted with six large pearls.
It dates from Charles II

Hong Kong signs by Henry Steiner

A writer once expressed his first delight at seeing the neon signs of Hong Kong which seemed to him Confucius written in letters of flame. And his subsequent disappointment at discovering that these were advertisements for a variety of pills, ointments, balms, and laxatives.

Hong Kong is physically small, with a population of 4,000,000, of whom 99% are Chinese. Some of its areas are the most congested in the world and its land prices are the highest anywhere. The economy is based on a pure form of *laissez-faire* capitalism. A free port with no real natural resources, Hong Kong lives by trade. Because of the crowding, its business life is extremely competitive and volatile. Its weather is subtropical with little rain and the people spend much time outdoors in the city streets; strong typhoons are occasional visitors. These factors are reflected in the signs of Hong Kong, some of which are shown on the following pages.

There are still many traditional signs hanging in Hong Kong but these are wrongly respected for their antiquity rather than for their handsome clarity which outshines most of the 'modern' creations. There is nothing exotic in this: the original gold on red wooden Woolworth's signs were not only nicer, but clearer than their plastic descendants.

Conceived of as occupying an imaginary square, each Chinese character stands for one word. Many characters retain their pictographic or ideographic origins. They are normally drawn with a brush and read down from the upper right or horizontally in either direction. (The Communist Chinese and the Japanese have begun to standardize horizontal left to right reading but no such system applies to the Overseas Chinese.) This flexibility of adaptation combined with the fierce competitiveness of local business and the rather diffident attitude of Government in respect to zoning restrictions has led to a condition in Hong Kong which can best be called a 'typographic explosion'. There are more signs and letters per square yard in Hong Kong than anywhere else in the world. The signs obliterate architecture, the sky, and seem to be struggling for survival with the very residents of Hong Kong. That their foreign nature renders the signs illegible and 'interesting' to a non-Chinese, does not make the problem less acute. The streets shown are normal streets. It is as though a combination of the signs of Times Square and Piccadilly Circus were spread all over an entire city.

The signs of Hong Kong today serve as a sobering example of what can happen without control and enlightened supervision of typography in the street.

20

Breton fishing boat numerals

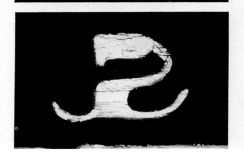

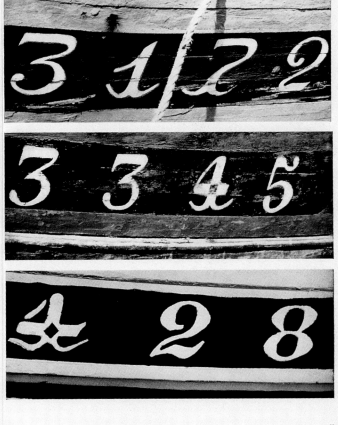

25

Below left: *Typographica*,
NS no. 12, December 1965.
Design and photograph:
Spencer.
Below: *Typographica*,
NS no. 13, June 1966.
Design: Spencer.
Photograph: Henry Steiner.

'THE POSSIBILITY OF NEW RELATIONS BETWEEN WORDS AND IMAGES IS SELDOM PURSUED ON A CONSTRUCTIVE PUBLIC SCALE. NO EDITOR YET THINKS OF A PHOTOGRAPHIC LIBRARY AS A POSSIBLE *VOCABULARY*; NOBODY DARES TO PLACE IMAGES AS PRECISELY IN RELATION TO A TEXT AS A QUOTATION WOULD BE PLACED; FEW WRITERS YET THINK OF USING PICTURES TO MAKE THEIR ARGUMENT.'

JOHN BERGER, 'WORDS AND IMAGES', 1965

series of images unbroken by long texts to build visual narratives. Brownjohn's is a 31-page marathon of acute visual wit, in which London is re-seen 'not so much as architecture as three-dimensional typography' – much of it falling apart. Examples of this visual street 'music' are juxtaposed with recent examples of mainly American design employing similar tropes to show how a scavenging eye can discover in the city's fabric sources of a new sensibility and aesthetic. In later issues, Spencer pursued his interest in the sometimes chaotic visual energy of the urban scene by presenting photographic stories on improvised uses of the symbol devised for the Fourth Centenary of Rio de Janeiro; arrows and fists in the street; Hong Kong street signs; and Spanish street lettering. Spencer's collection of pictures of Breton fishing boat numerals are a rare departure from the captivating clamour of the city street.

Fundamental to Spencer's thinking about photographic series, and his use of them in *Typographica*, was the book *Let Us Now Praise Famous Men*, James Agee's and Walker Evans's documentary record of poor sharecropper families living in the American South.[22] Spencer had seen Evans's work in the late 1940s and assimilated its lessons before returning to it as a committed photographer in the 1960s. The book begins, even before its title page, with a series of photographs of sharecroppers, children, wooden shacks, fields, animals, empty interiors, a gas station, a grave; there are no captions or commentaries – no typography at all. In one photograph, which Spencer singles out in conversation, a collection of old calendars forms a mournful wall-collage above a crude wooden mantlepiece. In the photograph on the opposite page, two dog-eared photos of an old woman and a group of children are nailed to a wall. The viewer – the *reader* – is left to decide what these images mean and how they relate to others in a sequence that has been ordered with great deliberation by Evans. Spencer explains:

> . . . this is one of the things I was talking to John Berger about subsequently, about the idea of making a statement through a series of photographs: not illustrating a text, not even requiring captions, in fact probably better and stronger if they are presented without captions because if you look at the images, you don't really need the captions . . . it tends to weaken the statement because I think people looking at it will first form an impression from the photograph, and then read the caption, which may in fact contradict their own interpretation, or modify it.[23]

Spencer had first met John Berger (b. 1926), then working as art critic for the *New Statesman*, in 1953, when they were both invited on a cultural tour of the Soviet Union. In April 1963, Berger wrote to Spencer thanking him for a letter in which Spencer had evidently mentioned 'photography in series' in response to an article by Berger about photography: 'I wish I could add a P.S. to the article – for it is an important point that you make', writes Berger.[24] In a second letter to Spencer, later in the year, Berger returns to the theme:

John Berger, writer and critic, c.1962

This is my private world.

I am not presenting it to be judged or evaluated – 'that's good, that's not so good, that's been done before'. Only to be experienced. I am presenting it with the demand that it should be *looked at*, without preconceptions or prejudice. You can't (or shouldn't) try to judge another human being's personal world. You can only try to understand it by experiencing it. Or you can ignore it.

I haven't tried to produce a new or an old gimmick, or another kind of free expression or collage. Also, the part of my world that you can see here is not simply pure design. Although it must contain some elements of design, its basic governing principle is *content*.

For me the camera is not a means to an end – the finished photograph. Photographs themselves are a means to an end, elements of a whole. Each element has to be placed in relation to the others and to the whole in such a way that it becomes (for me) true. Falseness lies mainly in the seduction of design and the desire for effect.

Content or truth remains to a great extent in the eyes of the beholder. It would be impossible to include here anything so definite or obvious as 'a politician', 'a slum' – impossible to pass judgements, quote morals or messages. I have used each picture because it contains an equal amount of precision and vagueness.

To my eyes, a certain picture may have a definite content. But what has that to do with your eyes?

Jane Gate

Typographica, NS no. 7, May 1963, 273 × 825 mm. Fold-out page, recto and verso, for 'This is my private world . . .' Text and photographs: Jane Gate.

... I agree with you about the importance of pictures in sequence – and maybe too this is just at the beginning of its possibilities. As soon as you have sequence, you have time passing, and as soon as you have that – you have the necessity for poetry.[25]

Spencer had sent Berger a copy of *Typographica*, NS no. 7, containing an article by a young photographer, Euan Duff, on 'Thematic photography' and a series of 21 photographs by Duff of children and their teacher at the Gospel Oak School, London, designed by Spencer as a 16-page booklet to maximize the sense of sequence. Duff's series, shot during 1961 and 1962, shares an acknowledged relationship with the Southam Street slum photographs of Roger Mayne – 57 of which were published, in 1961, in Theo Crosby's *Uppercase*.[26] Duff himself refers to Mayne's 'thematic technique' in *Typographica*, while six photographs by Mayne are also included in the issue.[27] He describes how he takes many pictures to capture his impression of a situation, discovering in the process incidents of greater or lesser significance. In his letter to Spencer, Berger responded to Duff's article and photographs with great enthusiasm:

I have the sense of knowing that schoolmaster – as though I had read a long short story about him . . . I even have an idea of how he puts his clothes on in the morning – and certainly a very distinct impression of his voice. The vividness with which he and his teaching methods and his attitude to children and his sense of the significance of being a teacher – come across, is in direct ratio, it seems to me, to Duff's own modesty and maturity. . . .[28]

Below: *Typographica*, NS no. 7, May 1963. Spread from 'Thematic photography', showing inset 16-page booklet, 124 x 203 mm. Text and photographs: Euan Duff. Booklet design: Spencer.

Opposite: *Uppercase*, no. 5, 1961, 178 x 282 mm. Spread from 'Portrait of Southam Street' by Roger Mayne. Publisher: Whitefriars.

He originated the term 'decisive moment', which he described as 'the simultaneous recognition in a fraction of a second of the significance of an event, as well as of a precise formal organization which brings that event to life'.
Cartier-Bresson's great photographs are complete and unquestionable, but his

The logical conclusion for me is to build up those more limited pictures in order to show the whole situation in detail, and to use the one successful picture either by itself or as a climax to the thematic development. Roger Mayne used a thematic technique with his series of photographs 'Portrait of Southam Street', published by

alter the meaning of that situation. The final result can never, I think, be called 'realism' or 'truth'. It is only what one individual felt significant at one point in time. I have quite often gone to photograph a subject with a set idea towards it but, later, while studying the results, I discover that what comes over as important is completely different from any original conception. When photographing I am able to concentrate intensely, and this helps a deeper understanding of the subject.
I have to take many pictures to capture any impression of a situation. While working, I continually move around, altering my viewpoint, my focus, and my composition in an attempt to discover incidents of greater or different significance. In order to photograph one particular relationship I often also cover many different situations. To obtain one successful picture I therefore take many other, more limited pictures. Some of these will be good, perhaps showing more clearly some minor aspects of the original subject.

Euan Duff is 23. He is married, with one step-child. He studied commercial photography at the London School of Printing for three years and freelanced in photo-journalism for two years. He now spends most of his time working on thematic developments for books, etc. (and on propagating this use of photography), and he also teaches photography at the South West Essex Technical College, School of Art. His interest in education as a subject developed out of watching mothers with their children. Depressed by the apparent lack of understanding, he visited a local State primary school, at Gospel Oak, to see how professionals coped with similar problems. He was immediately impressed by the atmosphere he found there and he took photographs of several classes, including Class 4 under Mr Deadman. A selection of these photographs is reproduced in the facing inset. Some of the opinions of Mr R. B. Lendon, the School's progressive headmaster, are printed overleaf. (These views are not necessarily those of the London County Council.)

50

51

Berger goes on to mention a close friend in Geneva, Jean Mohr, who was also impressed by Duff's work. In 1964, Berger and Spencer met at Spencer's Blomfield Road house. Berger showed him examples of Mohr's photography, as well as some photographs of his own. As he describes in his book with Mohr, *Another Way of Telling* (1982), Berger contacted the photographer to learn how to use a camera, so he could take a series of photographs 'which would accompany, and be interchangeable with, a sequence of love poems'.[29] For two years he took hundreds of pictures. While in London he proposed the idea of publishing the project in *Typographica* and Spencer agreed. In October 1964, Berger wrote again, in response to Spencer's suggestion that the nine poems be printed on transparent paper, so that the photographs could be seen behind them. He agreed 'so long as they are *easily* legible', but expressed a reservation:

> . . . by arranging them in this way we are bound to lose one thing: which is the feeling of the photographs being a visual sequence. (The poems will stay a sequence because their progression is far more obvious and cerebral.) Could we not therefore print first one page (perhaps opposite the Introduction?) of all the photographs together in sequence – almost as though they were contact prints – and without of course any text at all? The photographs filling the whole page. What do you think? Also I feel myself that it would give the reader–viewer a clue to the kind of scale of subject involved – like a visual table of contents.[30]

Berger added a thumbnail diagram to show the layout of the sequence – three rows 'reading' left to right. In the published

poem-sequence, titled *At Remaurian*, Spencer honoured this request. The nine short poems, presented as a separate booklet attached by a thread, are printed in black ink on a transparent overlay which mutes the accompanying black and white photograph; the two are first seen as a unity. The poems are legible enough to be read in this way, suffused by Berger's soft, dreamlike images of stone walls, grass, trees, the distant sea and the naked body of his beloved, or they can be lifted clear of the photographs to achieve an effect closer to a conventional page. The photographs, taken near Nice and Lacoste, can be studied through the veil of the overlay or seen directly. Berger explains in a note that photographs and poems both form a sequence. Sometimes he began with the photograph, sometimes with the poem; whichever it was, he did not start the poem with the photograph in mind, or look for a subject to accompany a poem: 'I have no opinion, therefore, about which should be seen first.'[31] Each sequence could also be considered separately; the approach taken is up to the reader.

The sequence of photographs is repeated within Berger's accompanying article, where it occupies roughly two-thirds of a page. Spencer has staggered the layout to encourage the reader's eye to scan the image-sequence horizontally. The repetition seems unnecessary, however, a loss of nerve after the openness and complexity of the alternative readings offered by the booklet. It allows the viewer to apprehend the sequence as an instant totality and to make more rapid connections between images, but this can

my own temperament and aptitudes, my loyalties have been divided between word and image. As a boy I painted pictures and wrote poems and stories in equal numbers.

At art school (to which I went in order to forgo the chance of attending an academic university) I painted, mostly, bad literary paintings and wrote static, visually descriptive pieces in prose and verse.

When I left art school I painted less anecdotal pictures – influenced in turn by Chagall, Soutine and Léger: but earned my living by talking about art.

A little later by writing art-criticism I learned to think historically and to choose words as though they were arrows which had to find their target. As the difficulties of thinking and writing became my primary conscious concern, my primary reality became the visual one.

It was not until quite recently (five or six years ago) that I began to realize that the idea of a 'divided loyalty' was false. Probably it was simply the experience of working for

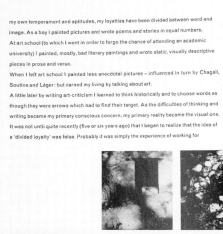

television and becoming creatively conse... *image* which first suggested some kind...

After I had... *live:* for...

JOHN BERGER   AT REMAURIAN

...taken about 100

...mountains.

...points may be helpful. The photographs, no less ...sequence: the tempo or measure of this sequence is much ...and more contemplative than that of a film – but it is just as much related to time passing.

Sometimes I took and printed the photograph first; sometimes I began writing the poem first. Whichever happened, I never began the poem with the photograph in my mind, or looked for a subject to photograph for the sake of the poem. I have no opinion, therefore, about which should be seen first. They are concerned with different facets of the same reality and whichever appears first depends on the reader's direction of approach. Each whole sequence might even be considered separately. Both represent two variations (each involving a different discipline and medium) on the theme of metamorphosis (landscape into flesh, male into female, and vice versa). Such metamorphoses themselves represent variations which are essential to the process of being seen. On at least one level the subject of the work is *sight*.

46

47

my own temperament and aptitudes, my loyalties have been divided between word and image. As a boy I painted pictures and wrote poems and stories in equal numbers.

At art school (to which I went in order to forgo the chance of attending an academic university) I painted, mostly, bad literary paintings and wrote static, visually descriptive pieces in prose and verse.

When I left art school I painted less anecdotal pictures – influenced in turn by Chagall, Soutine and Léger: but earned my living by talking about art.

A little later by writing art-criticism I learned to think historically and to choose words as though they were arrows which had to find their target. As the difficulties of thinking and writing became my primary re...

It was not until quite recently (five or six years... a 'divided loyalty' was false. Probably it was s...

III
At the nocturnal level of the hand,
Herbs must always grow
Leaf of my last
But early enough
And upright
Following in the wake of the trees
I have felt again at the veil of my wrist
Webs breaking
Till every connection of the night is severed
And single I step forward to become
The honey-coloured flecks
On the iris of the first-comer's eye,

television and becoming creatively... *image* which first suggested som...

After... *Clive:* for

...taken about 100 ...mountains.

...two points may be helpful. The photographs, no less ...in a sequence: the tempo or measure of this sequence is much ...er and more contemplative than that of a film – but it is just as much related to time passing.

Sometimes I took and printed the photograph first; sometimes I began writing the poem first. Whichever happened, I never began the poem with the photograph in my mind, or looked for a subject to photograph for the sake of the poem. I have no opinion, therefore, about which should be seen first. They are concerned with different facets of the same reality and whichever appears first depends on the reader's direction of approach. Each whole sequence might even be considered separately. Both represent two variations (each involving a different discipline and medium) on the theme of metamorphosis (landscape into flesh, male into female, and vice versa). Such metamorphoses themselves represent variations which are essential to the process of being seen. On at least one level the subject of the work is *sight*.

46

47

The following text appears within the reproduced spread (pages 46–47 of the original booklet):

my own temperament and aptitudes, my loyalties have been divided between word and
image. As a boy I painted pictures and wrote poems and stories in equal numbers.

At art school (to which I went in order to forgo the chance of attending an academic
university) I painted, mostly, bad literary paintings and wrote static, visually descriptive
pieces in prose and verse.

When I left art school I painted less anecdotal pictures – influenced in turn by Chagall,
Soutine and Léger: but earned my living by talking about art.

A little later by writing art-criticism I learned to think historically and to choose words as
though they were arrows which had to find their target. As the difficulties of
writing became my primary conscious concern, my primary

It was not until quite recently (five or six ye
a 'divided loyalty' was false. Probably it was

television and becoming creative
first suggested so

Clive : for
before
were

were taken about 100
on mountains.

two points may be helpful. The photographs, no less
a sequence: the tempo or measure of this sequence is much
and more contemplative than that of a film – but it is just as much related to
time passing.

Sometimes I took and printed the photograph first; sometimes I began writing the poem
first. Whichever happened, I never began the poem with the photograph in my mind, or
looked for a subject to photograph for the sake of the poem. I have no opinion, therefore,
about which should be seen first. They are concerned with different facets of the same
reality and whichever appears first depends on the reader's direction of approach. Each
whole sequence might even be considered separately. Both represent two variations
(each involving a different discipline and medium) on the theme of metamorphosis
(landscape into flesh, male into female, and vice versa). Such metamorphoses
themselves represent variations which are essential to the process of being seen. On at
least one level the subject of the work is *sight*.

46   47

hardly be counted a gain in a work that Berger intends the reader-
viewer to absorb slowly: 'the tempo or measure of this sequence is
much slower and more contemplative than that of a film – but it is
just as much related to time passing'.[32] Spencer says that although
he does not object to the repetition, he probably would not have
done it without Berger's suggestion (it does mean, however, that
the article will make at least partial sense should the booklet
become detached from the issue). It may be that Berger was not
able to visualize fully the effect that Spencer had in mind.[33] As it is,
his literary and artistic intentions, as described in *Typographica*,
were fully realized in Spencer's design of *At Remaurian*. By paying
such close attention to the material form in which the poems and
photographs are presented, Spencer brought another level of
signification to the project, imbuing it with an atmosphere of
reverent contemplation which is not only visual but tactile.

By the time *At Remaurian* was published in *Typographica*, Berger
was already at work with Jean Mohr on *A Fortunate Man* (1967),
a meditation in photographs and words on the life and philosophy
of a country doctor. In *Ways of Telling*, his critical study of Berger,
Geoff Dyer suggests that in its combination of text and image
A Fortunate Man is 'a new "kind" of book', the only real precedent
for which is Agee's and Evans's *Let Us Now Praise Famous Men*.[34]
Dyer believes that the reason this 'pivotal work' has received so
little critical attention is that for all its literary subtlety it does not
fall into the privileged category of fiction. It may also be because
it integrates photography and text with a sensitivity that remains

Above and opposite:
***Typographica*, NS no. 11,
June 1965. Spread from
'Words and images',
showing the *At Remaurian*
booklet, 138 × 175 mm. Text,
poems and photographs:
John Berger. Booklet
design: Spencer.**

83

highly unusual. Literary critics are, on the whole, neither inclined nor equipped to address the visual to the degree needed to engage fully with such a project.[35] Dyer himself does not discuss *At Remaurian*, although the experience of working on it was clearly important to the development of Berger's ideas about word and image. His decision to make a photographic document of a doctor's life in the community is surely not unconnected to his (and Mohr's) reactions to Duff's photographs of the teacher and his class published in *Typographica*.

'Words and images', Berger's article written to accompany and contextualize *At Remaurian*, is one of the key texts published in the second series. It is significant as a summary of the central ideas – manifest and latent – of the *Typographica* project, but important, too, for the way that it points forward to the later concerns and achievements of Berger and others working at the boundaries of the verbal and visual, the textual and photographic. 'Recent numbers of *Typographica* have shown how the image and the word are breeding,' Berger begins.[36] Artists are bringing together what is seen and what is written in new ways, using concrete poetry, Pop Art, agit-prop and the 'happening'. Television, pictorial journalism, advertising and new educational needs are also changing the established balance between word and image. He describes how the experience of working in television had overcome his sense of a 'divided loyalty' between text and picture, and had given him an understanding of the synthesis possible in a 'speaking image'.[37] Berger went on to find other ways

of making the image bear witness. His television series *Ways of Seeing* (1972), devised with Michael Dibb, fulfils all the demands he had made in *Typographica* for a constructive use of the (photographic) image – as vocabulary, quotation and argument. In *Another Way of Telling*, he returns to ideas about photographic sequence that had also preoccupied Spencer as photographer and editor. The book includes a complex, wordless narration of an old woman's reflections on her life, created by Berger and Mohr from Mohr's photographs.[38]

In 'Words and images', Berger criticizes much of what passes through mass media as trivial and false. If photographic images (and their digital simulations) now dominate in mass media and popular culture – in advertising, television, pop promos, computer games, the Hollywood blockbuster – this is hardly as a result of the critical thinking implied by Berger's new vocabulary of images. Away from the 'isolated artists' he imagines working inevitably on a very small scale, the anticipated critical synthesis of word and image remains the exception, particularly in print. While it is at the very least questionable whether the new relations between text and image that Berger and Spencer called for in *Typographica* have ever been adequately achieved on a 'constructive public scale', this is certainly what they realized, with great delicacy of feeling, in *At Remaurian*. Here, and in Spencer's other imaginative fusions of photography and design, the magazine made a significant contribution to its readers' education in the possibilities of the speaking image.

84

Below: *A Fortunate Man* by John Berger and Jean Mohr, 1967, 208 × 310 mm. Consecutive spreads from a sequence. Photographs: Jean Mohr. Design: Gerald Cinamon. Publisher: Allen Lane, The Penguin Press.

Opposite and pages 86–9: *Typographica*, NS no. 12, December 1965. Sequence of spreads from 'Emphatic fist, informative arrow' by Edward Wright, with photographs by Spencer. The sequence ends on a single, left-hand page. The first page, with text only, is not shown.

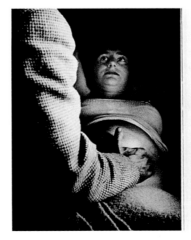

arrows of the American Indians were not a threat in the eastern States by that time. However simple in detail and silhouette, the arrow on a weathervane is a representation which has been found and assembled, whereas in modern traffic situations the arrow must be an informative pointer shaped to give a phased message to a moving target approaching it from several directions. The sign on the highway is really not an arrow at all; it is a diagram which can change direction and be read from a distance at windscreen level. We can call them arrows because 'arrow' now means a certain kind of sign.

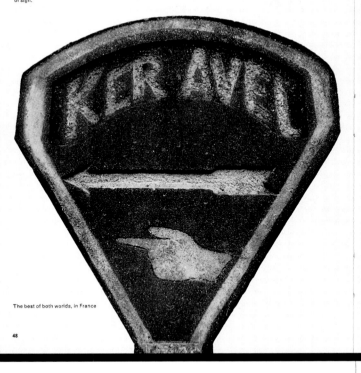

The best of both worlds, in France

Elias Canetti: *Crowds and Power*
(Eng. trans. Gollancz 1960):

The first thing that strikes one about a command is that it initiates action. An extended finger, pointing in a certain direction, can have the effect of a command: all that seems to be involved is initiation of some definite action, with movement in one given direction. The determination of direction is especially important; reversal or deflection should be felt as equally inadmissible.

… Every command consists of *momentum* and *sting*. The momentum forces the recipient to act, and to act in accordance with the content of the command; the sting remains behind in him.

… This relationship to the horse plays a decisive part in the command-economy of man, but among the Mongols there is another important factor. This is the *arrow*, the exact image of the original, non-domesticated command.
An arrow is hostile; it is meant to kill. It travels straight through space.

Arrows on the wall, in Italy

The arrow at ground level

The arrow leads the way...
to bungalows in Sicily,
to bunkers in Munich,
to a bank in Mayfair

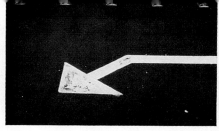

Arrows for pedestrians, cyclists, motorists – and flyers

Arrows of information and invitation

Emphatic fist, informative arrow

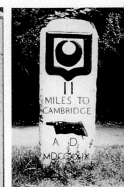

61

Private and public fists

62

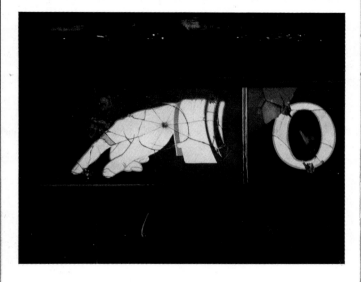

JEHOVAH'S
WITNESSES
TIMES OF MEETINGS
SUN. ⏜ 3·15
TUE. ⏜ 7·15
THUR. ⏜ 6·30

64

Variations on a theme in France

PENETRATION

PENETRATION

PENETRATION

PENETRATION

TION   PEN
ATION PENETI
NETPETRATI
PENETRATION

WASH
UP!
WASH

A MOIST TOWELETTE

FORD & C

s, Auctioneers & Estat

s, LINCO LN'S

ILBORN 3177

The photographs and designs juxtaposed on these and the following pages show the similarity that exists between primitive and accidental street typography, and purposeful typography produced by contemporary designers.

Top left and left: Disintegration quick, disintegration slow. A graphic piece of road-laying adds impact to the word of command. Marks and Co. get down to business at street level. And an experimental advertisement uses the same technique to illustrate a medical salve that penetrates muscle tissue. Opposite: Ribbed glass makes an apt symbol of a straight sign. And the designer again takes his technique from his streetscape.
A wrap-around notice becomes the mother of invention in package design where the word wraps around the pack like the product round the face.
Bad word spacing can happen. Or it can be designed.

me trotyp o graphersinco rporated2 7west2 4thstr eetnewyor k10telep honewat kins9- 6 290
metrot ypograph ersinc orpo rated27w est24t hstre etnewy ork1 0telephone watk ins9-62 90
metroty pograp hersincor po rated2 7we st24thstr eet newyor k10t elep honewatkin s9-6290
metrot ypog raphersincorpora ted2 7west24ths treet newy ork10te lephon ewat kins9 - 6290
m et rotypographersinc orpor ated27 west24t hstreetne wyork1 0tele phone watk ins9-62 90
metrotypog raphersinc orporat ed2 7west2 4thstree tnewyork10te lepho ne watk in s 9-6290
met rotypog raphe rsincor porated27 w est24t hstreetn ewyork10tel ephonew atkins 9-6 290
me trotyp o graphersinc orpor ated27west2 4 thstr ephonewatkin s9 -6290
metrotypograp hersinc orpora ted27we st24ths treet n ew york10t elepho ne watkins9-629 0
met roty pograph ersin corpora t ed27west 24thstreetnewyo rk10tele phone watkins 9- 6290
metroty pogr aphersincor pora ted27w est24t hst reet newyo rk 1 0telephonewatkins 9-6290
m et rotypog raph ersincorporated2 7wes t24th streetne wyork10t elephon ew atkins9-629 0
metrot ypogr aphersinc orpora ted2 7west2 4ths treetn ewy ork10tel ephonewat kin s9-6290
me trotyp o graphersincorpora ted 2 7west24thst reetnew york1 0 telephonewa tkins9 -6290
metr otypo graphersinco rpora ted27wes t24t streetn ewy ork10tele phonew atkin s 9-6290
me troty pographersi ncorpora ted 2 7west 24t hstreetnewyo rk1 0telepho ne watkins9-6290
metro typographers incorporated 27 west 24th street new york 10 telephone watkins 9-6290
metrotypographer sincor p orated2 7 west2 4thstreetney or k1 0 tel ephone atkins9-6290
met rotypog raphersinc orpor a ted27 west24 thst reetnewyork 10teleph one watkins9-629 0
metrot ypogr aphersincorpo rated2 7west 24thstreetn ewyork 10t eleph onewat kins9 - 6290
me trotyp o graphersinco rporated2 7west2 4thstr eetnewyor k10telep honewat kins9- 62 90

Above and pages 91–7:
Typographica, NS no. 4,
December 1961. Sequence of
spreads from 'Street level'
by Robert Brownjohn. The
street photographs, mostly
shot by Brownjohn, are
interspersed with examples
of graphic work by
colleagues: BCG, Bob Gill,

Colin Forbes, Alan Fletcher,
David Enock, Tony Palladino
and Stanley Eisenman.
Not shown are the first
page, with text only, and
last page, showing a busy
street scene, with a man
bearing a sign on his back
saying 'Almost blind'.

THE PHOTOGRAPHS . . . WERE HARVESTED ON ONE TRIP ROUND LONDON.
THE THINGS THEY SHOW HAVE VERY LITTLE TO DO WITH DESIGN, APART FROM
ACHIEVING ITS OBJECT. THEY SHOW WHAT WEATHER, WIT, ACCIDENT, LACK OF
JUDGEMENT, BAD TASTE, BAD SPELLING, NECESSITY, AND GOOD LOUD REPETITION
CAN DO TO PUT A SORT OF MUSIC INTO THE STREETS WHERE WE WALK.'
ROBERT BROWNJOHN, 'STREET LEVEL', 1961

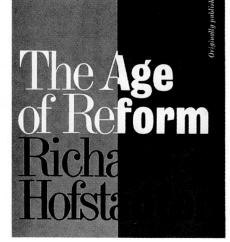

Left: Second-hand fencing on a building site achieves a fragmentation of letter forms (Photo by Don Foster), and the typographer does the same thing with a greetings-card. Then Colin Forbes goes even further on a dust-jacket.
Right: Fresh paint draws a sharp line between neighbours. And a designer draws the same line through history.

Originally publish

The Age of Re**form**
Richa
Hofsta

Type distorts significantly.
Type distorts purposefully for under-water fishing; repetitively like drinking Dubonnet; coarsely on a sack of potatoes; questionably about specialists. And type distorts into motion behind a piece of crinkled glass.

32

33

34

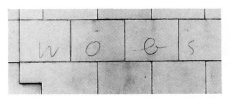

Terrain rears its pigeon-holed head to
confuse. Fifteen and sixteen and one
hundred and sixteen, truly searching
for paradise; the vertical treatment of an
advertisement illustrates typesetting
finesse; and David Enock's letterhead
obeys the rules of business machines
and spaces itself with a mechanical
ugliness.

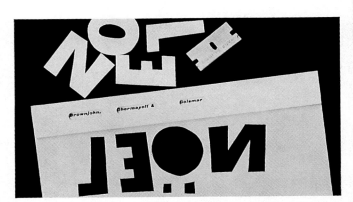

Repetition: the hardest, simplest way
to sell. Just say it again and again and
again and again and again.

BANG THE BOMB

architectural
& engineering

N E W S

1960NE

There is always room for the lazy soul
making his quick addition to the message.

41

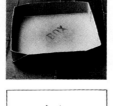

PSYCHO

Robert Bloch
An Inner Sanctum Mystery

RADESMEN ENTRANCE

ENTERTAINMENT

CLOSED / OPEN

PREMISES CLOSING DOWN
FOR REBUILDING

Type can illustrate hard. A sword in a
hand swipes three (photo by David
Bailey); the vintner's E is properly
tipsy; Tony Palladino's *Psycho* is word
and picture in one. Accidents will
happily happen for they emphasize,
crystallize, distort, excite, and inform.
The public must be told that radesmen
entrance. How else will it know?

42

43

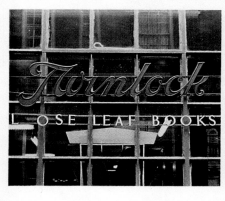 

Juxtaposition, accidental or designed, adds meaning and helps a message to illustrate itself. Nothing could be more closed than a locked lockshop. Nothing could be less open than a thricelocked door. Loose leaves ought to be loose, accessories ought to be needed and there's always more time for a signwriter's quick nack if he leaves the job unfinished.

Brownjohn Chermayeff & Geismar
An Exhibition of Graphic Design
The Composing Room: Gallery 303
130 West 46th St., New York City
Showing: July 15th to July 31st

The exhibition notice only composed itself after folding unrelated letters over more of the same, printed on glassine. Lost property, like charity, begins at home, Rock's neighbour could only be Rolls, and it's very casual management that wants staff as casual as that. The Pollo alla Cacciatore was probably prethreequarterpared by Bob Gill's private secretary. Transvasin is still penetrating typographically, and the removal men who may be having second thoughts about the quality of their work are emphatic about the effectiveness of their removing. The sign removes itself almost completely. The hairdresser is so difficult to get at he just has to be good.

Left: Any statement can be either strengthened or denied. Rock supersedes cha-cha and starts a history of modern dance, land agents keep a good stock of their product on the first floor, bells are too new-fangled for antique dealers, holes let lighting through and there are more kinds of danger than one.
Drawing, above, for William Hayett Inc. by Bob Gill. Design for Sun Engraving Co Ltd by Alan Fletcher.

NODNOL ,ENAL DROFLIM ,ESUOH DROFLIM
1528 RAB ELPMET : ENOHPELET
gnikametalp ohtil/gnivargneotohp/gnipytortcele/gnittesepyt
SGNIHT TA KOOL UOY YAW REVEHCIHW
ECIVRES RUOY TA ERA [JVB]
DETIMIL YNAPMOC GNIVARGNE NUS EHT
NODNOL ,ENAL DROFLIM ,ESUOH DROFLIM
1528 RAB ELPMET :ENOHPELET
gnikametalp ohtil/gnivargneotohp/gnipytortcele/gnittesepyt
WHICHEVER WAY YOU LOOK AT THINGS
[JVB] ARE AT YOUR SERVICE
THE SUN ENGRAVING COMPANY LIMITED
MILFORD HOUSE, MILFORD LANE, LONDON
TELEPHONE: TEMPLE BAR 8251

David Enock makes impact for Impact, Bob Gill makes a noise for CAi, destitute shopkeepers make chaos for London. All the same trick but some do it better than others.
David Enock uses alphabet offcuts to make a name for sculptor Weinrib and Colin Forbes has good honest blockmaker's fun. Mr Gottlieb did the same thing long, long ago.

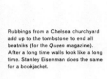

Passing Time
Michel Butor
Wednesday, August 6

Thursday, August 7

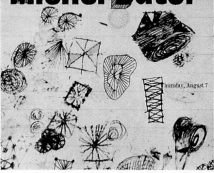

Rubbings from a Chelsea churchyard
add up to the tombstone to end all
beatniks (for the *Queen* magazine).
After a long time walls look like a long
time. Stanley Eisenman does the same
for a bookjacket.

S. PARMIGIANI

Numbers are numbers, Signor
Parmigiani says he sells gruyere and
the backs of signs make the same sort
of sense as neon at noon. Fenwick
ignores windows. No Parking ignores
automobiles. While-U-Wait ignores
time.

Letters drip to explain or obscure meaning. And letters weather to repel sporting types or to attract attention (Grillo by David Enock for a painter). Right: People are people. And they can't leave well alone.

The third dimension takes over for better or worse. The Pepsi P takes over Park Avenue and the same bottle caps that make an aptly designed cover for a house magazine make a street notice for an economical non-designer (photo by Herbert Spencer).

All photographs on pages 30–60 are by Robert Brownjohn, unless otherwise credited. Photographic processing by Robert Horner.

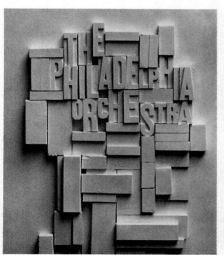

Typographica 3

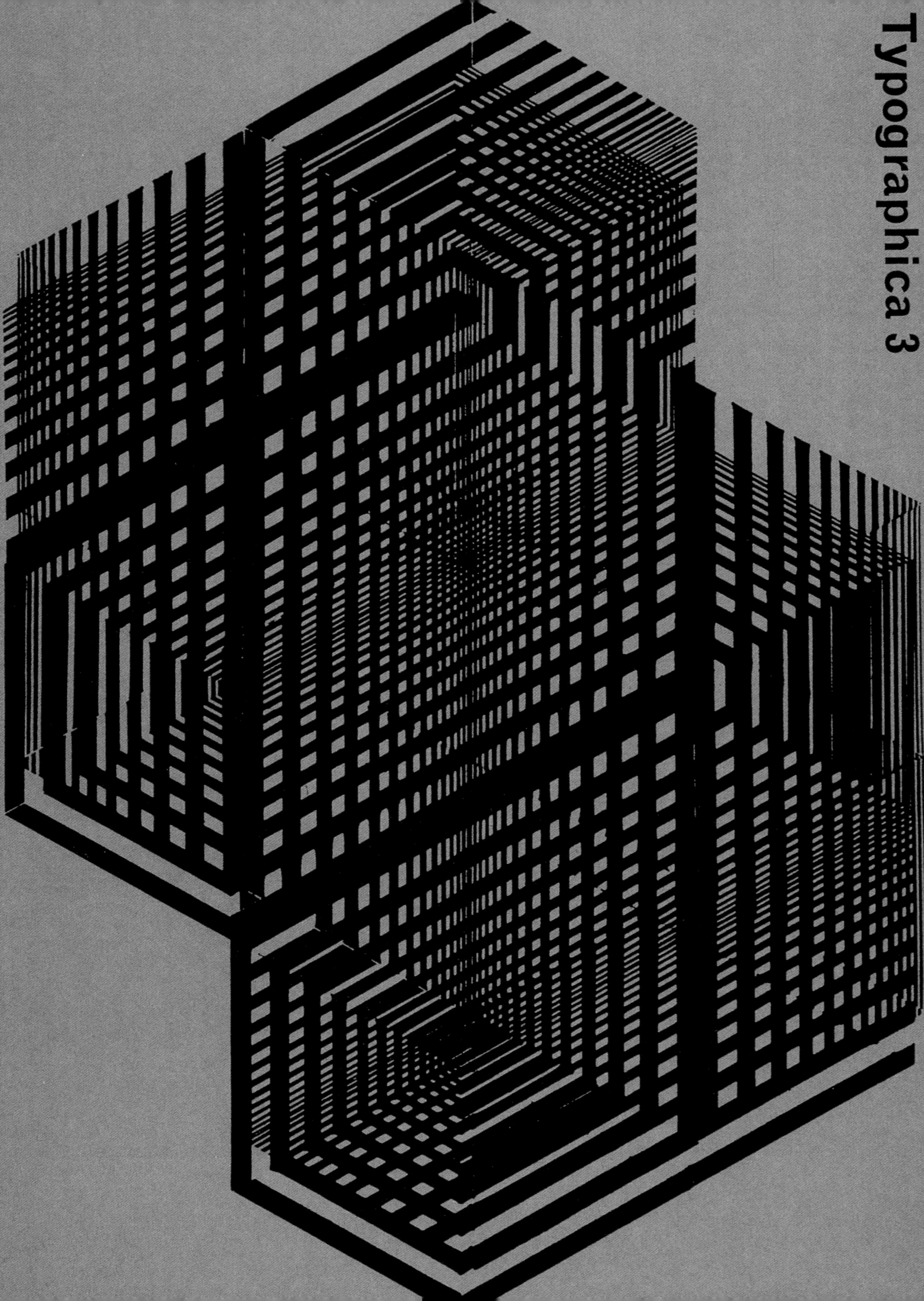

5.

Images and words
are breeding

Typographica, NS no. 3, June 1961. Design: Spencer, using an image by Diter Rot. (Slightly larger than original.)

In *Typographica*, NS no. 3, Spencer contrives a juxtaposition of articles which decisively establishes the magazine's breadth of sensibility and range of interests, while encapsulating the problematic richness of its treatment and view of typography throughout the series. Ken Garland's report on the 'typophoto' of the Swiss designers Armin Hofmann, Karl Gerstner, Siegfried Odermatt and Marcel Wyss is immediately followed in the issue's flatplan by Richard Hamilton's survey of Diter Rot's books. Garland, introducing his subject, explains that the integration of type and photo is 'one of the prime functions, perhaps *the* prime function of the graphic designer' backing up the contention with a portfolio of examples in which photography and typography are subordinated to the architecture of the page. Hamilton, meanwhile, prefaces a short preliminary discussion of the varieties of typography with the reminder that typography is more a craft than an art. The ≫→

typographer's job, he advises, is 'to present the ideas provided in the copy with sympathy and understanding. The best of typographers attempt no more, nor need they.'[1] Artists, however, can explore the visual form of the word, using type to 'reinforce poetic ideas' and 'create messages as much pictorial as literary'. Hamilton (b. 1922) is an artist with an unusually sympathetic view of design; but his concern here, before he moves on to discuss Rot's use of type as a 'medium of high art', is to delineate roles and establish defined limits for the graphic designer, even if the activities of artists have sometimes left a few 'dents' in his typographic vocabulary.

The reader (in most cases a designer) is left to make what he or she can of this juxtaposition. A continuity of interest and overlap of aesthetic concern is clearly implied by the articles' joint inclusion, in such close proximity; such conjunctions do not happen by accident in a publication as carefully directed, in all its details, as *Typographica* in its second series. Yet both writers sound a note of caution that verges on being a 'disclaimer'. Garland, equally anxious, on the design side, to establish clear limits to his discipline, doubts that a 'slap-dash shambles of unrelated types and photographs, however whimsical and evocative', can be called a design[2]; and this admonition is relatively mild compared to the routine diktats of the Swiss typography which is the subject of his article.

In fact, the book projects by Rot (1930–98) shown in Hamilton's article evince a comparable degree of technical rigour. Rot, says

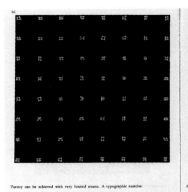
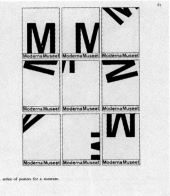

Above: *Graphic Design: Visual Comparisons* by Alan Fletcher, Colin Forbes and Bob Gill, 1963, 197 × 328 mm. Spread showing, on left, a page from *Bok 1956–59* by Diter Rot. Publisher: Studio Books.

Below: *Typographica*, NS no. 3, June 1961. Spread from 'The books of Diter Rot' by Richard Hamilton, with folding inset from *Bok 1956–59*. Opposite: *Typographica*, NS no. 3. Spread from 'Typophoto' by Ken Garland, showing designs by Siegfried Odermatt.

Siegfried Odermatt

Back and front cover and inside spread
of a leaflet for a corrugated board maker.

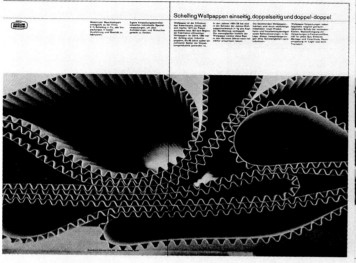

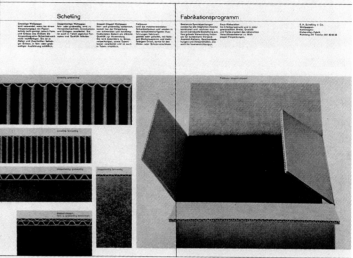

Schelling Wellpappen einseitig, doppelseitig und doppel-doppel

Schelling

Fabrikationsprogramm

inset and above:
s by Diter Rot from
59
in an edition of 400 copies

27

102 'THE GRAPHIC DESIGNER USING TYPE WILL NEED TO BE SOMETHING OF AN ARTIST BUT THE TYPOGRAPHER OF TODAY IS A LOGICIAN WHOSE JOB IS TO DISTRIBUTE GIVEN INFORMATION IN THE MOST RATIONAL WAY POSSIBLE.'

RICHARD HAMILTON, 'THE BOOKS OF DITER ROT', 1961

Hamilton, 'manipulates the limitations of the mechanics of modern print to construct his aesthetic'.[3] In *Bok 1956–59*, for instance, a single size of a single sanserif typeface is used, in lower case only. By restricting the range of units and concentrating on the plastic as opposed to semantic possibilities of the type material, Rot achieves a series of contrapuntal variations which, Hamilton suggests, form an 'Esperanto of the eye' capable of universal comprehension.

Spencer achieves a contrapuntal variation of his own with the editorial material. The Typophoto/Rot pairing is mirrored in the issue's flatplan by a second pairing. After Rot comes a primarily visual article of 11 pages about a series of advertisements and coloured wrappers for the Swiss daily newspaper *National Zeitung*

designed by Karl Gerstner and Markus Kutter, whose work has already featured in Garland's article. Gerstner and Kutter's austere geometrical type constructions for the ads immediately bring to mind Rot's type variations, while the folding pages used to show the wrappers are an elaboration, in material terms, of the folding pages included in the Rot article.

The final element of this carefully constructed editorial sequence is an article by Spencer on the American abstractionist Alcopley (Alfred Lewin Copley, 1910–92) whose drawings are a kind of wordless handwriting – 'Controlled, deliberate, yet free of alphabetic and symbolic restrictions' – that bears an obvious relation, despite the differences of aesthetic method, with Rot's non-semantic concerns.[4] The *National Zeitung*/Copley pairing

Opposite: *Typographica*,
NS no. 3, June 1961. Spread
from 'National Zeitung',
with a fold-out wrapper,
designed by Karl Gerstner
and Markus Kutter, for trial
copies of the Swiss
newspaper.
Right: *Typographica*,
NS no. 3. Spreads from
'The drawings of Alcopley'
by Spencer.

Alcopley   photograph by Fred Stein, New York

The Drawings of Alcopley   by Herbert Spencer

The drawings of Alcopley are handwriting without words. Controlled,
deliberate, yet free of alphabetic and symbolic restrictions, his fluid, vibrant
line – sometimes more delicate than a hair, sometimes as bold and abrupt
as the blood-spatter of a bullet – expresses a nervous, haunting rhythm.
Alcopley was born in Dresden in June 1910. He became an American
citizen in 1937. Under the name of Alfred Copley his scientific work, in the
fields of physiology and hematology, is well-known. But his drawings are
made, not as a form of self-conscious relaxation, but as a normal part of
his daily activity. He draws all the time: in cafés and at home, while
travelling and while waiting, at concerts and in lectures. Like a chain-
smoker's cigarette, Alcopley's pen is an almost permanent appendage of
his fingers and his pockets are full of little note-books – some, from Japan,
only an inch or two square. To look through any of these, selected at
random, is to understand the exceptional facility and fluency of his
draughtsmanship. All his drawings are made directly without revision or

Alcopley

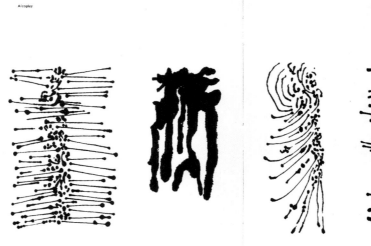

103

restates and amplifies the design/art juxtaposition of Typophoto/Rot, but despite the consistently fluid articulation in Spencer's design of these articles there is a much higher degree of formal divergence in the second pairing.

It would be three decades before designers using digital design tools would arrive independently at the possibilities of a non-semantic abstract 'typography' implicit in the drawings of an artist such as Alcopley.[5] That the formal implications of Rot's work were not, however, lost on at least some of *Typographica*'s readers can be seen in the book *Graphic Design: Visual Comparisons* (1963). Alan Fletcher, Colin Forbes and Bob Gill make explicit the comparison Spencer had implied through editorial juxtaposition by including two examples by Rot first seen

in *Typographica* alongside professional designs from Britain, the United States, France, Italy and Switzerland.[6] A 'typographic exercise' by Rot – their description suggests a teaching exercise rather than the 'high art' of Richard Hamilton – is contrasted with a poster series for the Swedish Moderna Museet in which the letter 'M' is rotated in a way reminiscent, at a pinch, of Rot's systematic mining of the compositional possibilities of b/d/p/q.[7]

Throughout the second series Spencer continued to explore, in parallel, the two worlds represented by the editorial pairings in *Typographica*, NS no. 3. They co-exist as possibilities in its pages, but at this early point in British graphic design's development nothing like a fusion is achieved. Fletcher, Forbes and Gill's interest in Rot cannot be taken as typical of the concerns of a design community rapidly establishing its professional presence in the early 1960s.

In the second series, Spencer published several heavily illustrated short profiles of contemporary designers who particularly interested him, but compared to a showcase for practising designers such as *Graphis* they are few in number and highly selective. The Italian designer Franco Grignani wrote to Spencer in 1958 – 'I do think that the line you follow is very near to mine and that your effort to lead graphic design toward an artistic expression is common to my aims' – and quotations from the letter were used by Alan Bartram for an article on Grignani in *Typographica*, NS no. 1.[8] In the following issue, Spencer published articles about the Swiss-Italian designer Max Huber and the New York firm Brownjohn, Chermayeff and Geismar, founded just three years earlier – the start of a fruitful association and friendship with Robert Brownjohn, who moved to London in the summer of 1960. Spencer's enthusiasm for particular designers occasionally led to a period of editorial collaboration – as with Max Bill in the early issues of the first series. Brownjohn went on to design the cover of NS no. 4, and to contribute two articles, 'Street level' and 'Sex and typography', featuring four design projects based on female anatomy. NS no. 6 includes a reproduction in reduced size of *Watching words move*, a 48-page 'typographic notebook' made in 1959 and 1960 by Brownjohn, Chermayeff and Geismar in which the typographic treatment of word-shapes demonstrates

Above: Robert Brownjohn, Ivan Chermayeff and Thomas Geismar, c. 1960. Below: *Typographica*, NS no. 2, December 1960. Spread from 'BCG', showing work by Ivan Chermayeff, left, and Brownjohn, Chermayeff and Geismar, right.

104

MODERN BANKING IS ELECTRONIC BANKING

From a full-page advertisement in *Fortune Magazine* for Transitron Electronics.
Opposite, poster for Brownjohn, Chermayeff, and Geismar's exhibition at the Composing Room, which makes use of scraps torn from envelopes in which the name of the partnership has been mis-spelt. Original in two colours.

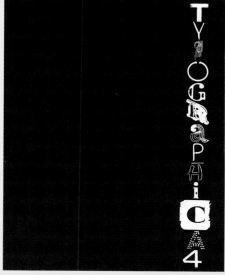

Top: *Typographica*,
NS no. 6, December 1962.
Opening spread from 'Pat
McAuliffe of Listowel' by
Bryan MacMahon, with
Watching words move
booklet by Brownjohn,
Chermayeff and Geismar,
140 × 115 mm.

Above: *Typographica*,
NS no. 4, December 1961.
Design: Robert Brownjohn,
using photographs of
illuminated letters.
Right: Spreads from
Watching words move,
compiled in 1959–60.

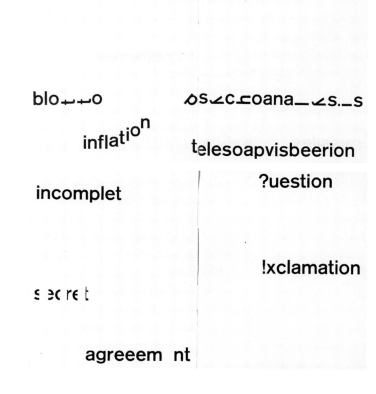

Top: Display panels at the 'Typography in Britain today' exhibition at Lund Humphries, Bedford Square, London, in May 1963. Three panels of work by Spencer, including ads for City Engraving, can be seen on the left.

Above: Front of folding catalogue for 'Typography in Britain today', 177 × 150 mm. Design: Spencer.

their linguistic content (i.e. 'addding' has an extra 'd', 'div id ing' is breaking apart).[9] Later in the new series, Germano Facetti introduced the work of the French designer Robert Massin, whose designs had been included – uncredited – in Facetti's article on French book clubs in OS no. 13.

As in the first series, it was an exhibition that allowed Spencer to make his most concerted gesture of support for the new design, concentrating this time on British examples. 'Typography in Britain today' was held at Lund Humphries' Bedford Square offices from 1 to 15 May 1963 and *Typographica*, NS no. 7 was published a month early to coincide with it. Thirty-seven designers were each invited to make a selection of their work and present it however they wished on three display panels. The issue includes biographies, photographs of most of those included and work by Tom Wolsey, Fletcher/Forbes/Gill, Alan Bartram, Romek Marber, Dennis Bailey, Gordon House, Robert Brownjohn, Edward Wright, George Daulby, John Denison-Hunt, Richard Hollis, George Mayhew, John Sewell, Leslie McCombie, and Spencer. Examples of advertising, magazines, book covers, corporate literature and poster design are shown. 'The practice of typography in Britain has undergone enormous changes during the past ten years,' Spencer notes in an upbeat introduction.[10] Printing has responded rapidly to the new climate that comes with a prosperous society and the role of the independent typographical designer is now accepted. Most designers attracted to typography in recent years have received formal typographic training at art school; this, and the typographer's rise in status, are perhaps the most significant developments. 'The "new typography" has established itself here, as elsewhere, because it has proved to be an effective vehicle for conveying contemporary ideas and messages in print.'[11]

'Typography in Britain today' brought together hundreds of examples of recent design work, but its thunder was stolen by other exhibitions and developments in the professional respresentation of British design. Moreover, there is something old-fashioned about the work's designation by Spencer as 'typographical design'. From the start of the decade, many of those in 'Typography in Britain today' increasingly described themselves as *graphic designers*. A group of like-minded young designers established the Association of Graphic Designers: London in 1960 to give additional legitimacy to the exhibition 'Graphic Design: London', held at the Time Life Building, which went on to attract more than 3,000 visitors. Among those involved in the association were Alan Fletcher, Colin Forbes, Dennis Bailey, George Daulby, George Mayhew, Derek Birdsall, Peter Wildbur and Tom Wolsey – all later included in Spencer's exhibition – and John Commander, art director at the printer Balding and Mansell. In 1963, Balding and Mansell published the book *17 Graphic Designers London*, with an introduction by Commander, featuring many of the same designers as 'Typography in Britain today' and some of the same designs.[12]

Above: *Typographica*, NS no. 7, May 1963. Exhibitors at 'Typography in Britain today'. The photographs are printed in silver metallic ink and the names are printed in red on the tissue paper overlay. Spencer is no. 20.

Below: *Typographica*, NS no. 7. Work included in 'Typography in Britain today' by Fletcher/Forbes/ Gill, on left, and Alan Bartram, on right.

IMAGES AND WORDS ARE BREEDING

In 1962, a new organization, the Designers and Art Directors Association (D&AD), was formed with the intention of organizing an exhibition in 1963. John Commander was elected chairman and 403 items of print and 38 films were selected from approximately 3,500 entries by the judging panel, which included Robert Brownjohn, Barry Trengrove, Germano Facetti, Tom Wolsey, Colin Forbes, Derek Birdsall, Romek Marber, David Collins, Ian Bradbery and Jock Kinneir (all, except for Brownjohn, members of the association).[13] The D&AD exhibition was held at the Hilton Hotel, London in June 1963, then shown at the IPEX show, Earls Court in July 1963, where it was seen by 25,000 visitors. In its July issue, *Design* devoted a major article to the D&AD show and the exhibition 'Graphics RCA: Fifteen years' work of the School of Graphic Design', held at the Royal College of Art from April to May 1963.[14] Spencer, on the other hand, made no mention of D&AD's formation or its imminent exhibition in his introduction to NS no. 7. *Design* did not get round to noticing the typography issue until six months after publication, when its reviewer criticized 'the fashion-ridden, gimmicky and often irrational work that passes as good design' – exemplified, for him, by Tom Wolsey's advertisement for the El Al airline – and accused the designers of only the most cursory attempts at typography.[15]

Spencer did not respond to Pop Art, or to the wave of Pop graphic design emanating from the Royal College of Art. For Mark Boxer, writing in the *Graphics RCA* catalogue, it was cause for celebration that design had at last found inspirations other than Mondrian and the Bauhaus. Pop might be 'instant nostalgia' but it possessed a 'spontaneous enjoyment of the phenomena of today, with a typographic and design style that has a wide future'.[16] Spencer took the opposite view. He felt that Pop 'hadn't the same relevance for typography, or at least I rather hoped it hadn't because it really rather contradicted much that was emerging in the typographic field at that time'.[17] Pop's kitsch revivalism and love of Victoriana (ironic or not) were not to his taste: 'it seemed to me to have that quality which I disliked about so much work that was done in England up to that time … there was always a kind of cosy jokiness which was rather provincial, I thought.'[18]

In his sympathies and interests, Spencer remained much closer to the Continent than to the US. He did not go to America until 1958, when he spoke at the New York Type Directors Club conference in Silvermine, Connecticut.[19] Work by several Americans was featured in the 'Purpose and Pleasure' exhibition, but the only other Americans published in *Typographica*'s first series were Rand and Lustig. Anne Massey, writing about the Independent Group (IG), makes a distinction between their approach to modernism – 'a starting point from which an analysis of culture was undertaken'[20] – and the approach taken by Roland Penrose and Herbert Read, founders of the ICA, where the IG's meetings took place. Penrose and Read retained a firm commitment to what they saw as the unbeatable

108   Below: *Ark*, no. 34, summer
1963, 269 × 219 mm. Design:
Melvyn Gill. Publisher:
The Royal College of Art,
London.
Below right: *Ark*, no. 34.
Text: Richard Hamilton.
Design and photograph:
Melvyn Gill.

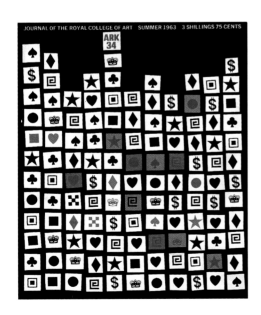

Motif, no. 10, winter 1962/3,
303 × 240 mm. Design:
Peter Blake. Publisher:
Shenval Press.

achievements of the pre-war European avant-garde. By its
second session, however, the IG was focusing almost exclusively
on American culture. Modernism was now identified with
America and Europe no longer led the avant-garde. In 1956,
Spencer saw 'This is Tomorrow' at the Whitechapel Art Gallery,
London, but although he appreciated the exhibition's fusion of
painting, graphics, architecture and industrial design, he did not
share the IG's fascination with consumerism and American
popular culture – as manifested in the exhibit featuring images
of Marilyn Monroe and Robbie the Robot.[21] Nor was he impressed,
in the 1950s, by American graphic design, which he felt to be
parochial and lacking in the rationale, logic and intellectual
discipline of the European design he had championed. His
tastes and allegiances had been shaped in the 1940s and 1950s
by the rigour of Constructivism and the vigour of abstraction
and *Typographica* featured work by both schools. Confronted
by the brash Pop graphics of the 1960s, he had much more in
common with the European modernism of Penrose and Read –
as the publication of *Pioneers of Modern Typography* in 1969
would confirm.

Pop was, as a result, peripheral to *Typographica. Ark*, positioned
on Pop's front line at the RCA, devoted whole issues to the Pop
sensibility. Issue 32, in summer 1962, was a compendium of
Pop gestures, from its cover collage, featuring a fairground
slot machine, Joker playing card and Victorian moustaches,
to art editor Brian Haynes's inset 'Kit of images' crammed with

'IS "POP" REALLY WITH IT, THEN? HE IS TOO MUCH WITH IT! FAR FROM BEING
A NORMAL CONSUMER OF EXPENDABLE GOODS HE KNOWS ABOUT ORIGINS AND
SOURCES; WORSE, HE WAS A MEMBER OF THE DREADED INDEPENDENT GROUP.
HE IS ONE OF THOSE WHO HAVE HELPED TO CREATE THE MENTAL CLIMATE
IN WHICH THE POP–ART PAINTERS HAVE BEEN ABLE TO FLOURISH IN ENGLAND.'
REYNER BANHAM, 'WHO IS THIS "POP"?' 1962

Right: *Typographica*,
NS no. 8, December 1963,
273 × 999 mm. Fold-out
inset for 'A rich man's
guide to bingo'. Text,
photographs and design:
Anthony Clift.

Below. *Typographica*,
NS no. 12, December 1965.
Spread from 'Art on the
assembly line' by Ann
Gould. The essay examines
the 'vicarious pleasure' of
clip art and its 'public
presentation of universal-
norm attitudes and
expressions'.

'Summats for now'

Not with this idea in mind, I enrolled at a bingo club in Cleethorpes, on the east coast of Lincolnshire, to try to unearth
what induces thousands of people nightly to abscond from television and spend at least eight shillings on one-and-a-half
hours of soporific number-calling, number-erasing, bingo-shouting fun. Fun?

The long line of cars outside the bingo halls may seem to suggest affluence. Not at all. They only reveal the hire-purchase
philosophy of the audience. In fact, the majority of the 'players' consist of head-scarved, hair-curlered, chain-smoking,
nicotine-fingered women between the ages of 23 and 65 – some with husbands or lovers teetering behind.

Five shillings membership fee and two shillings entrance fee admit one to dense smoke and piercing cacophony.

The setting: Cleethorpes' only theatre, metamorphosed. Emblazoned with Day-glo paint, neon lighting, fruit machines, and
banks of loud speakers and cheap prizes, it is once more a paying concern, but not, unfortunately, for the Theatre.

The four bingo cards necessary for the games are bought inside the hall for one shilling each. They vary in price from club to
club, and consist of a yellow card, a white card, and a salmon-coloured card, each used for five games, and a red card used
once for the jackpot game. Each game consists of a grid three squares deep by nine squares wide with fifteen numbers
permutated from one to ninety, dispersed, five along each line, within the grid.

The number-caller has a glass box containing ninety table-tennis balls, each with a number from one to ninety painted on it,
which are constantly blown about inside the box and forced, one at a time, up through a tube. They are plucked from the
other end of the tube by the caller who then shouts out the number accompanied by some phrase which rhymes with the
number – usually commercial, sometimes obscene. As the numbers are bawled out they are illuminated on a large board
behind the caller. The players cross out the corresponding numbers as they appear on their cards, and the first player to
have all the numbers on his card crossed out, calls out 'BINGO' (or more usually 'HOUSE', which is a hang-over from
'Housey-Housey', a similar game to bingo, often played in the home at Christmas). But those players who find themselves in
a position to shout out 'BINGO' are usually so overcome, in their moment of ecstasy, that they utter a diversity of grunts and
shouts.

The first three games of each card are for the completion of one line only, and are for small prizes. The last two games are
for the completion of the full card, referred to as a 'Full House'. The prizes are increased considerably.

Between each game, a few bars of a pop record, while the winner's card is being checked. A cigarette. Cup of tea. An ice
cream. Noise.

Instant silence. The caller begins.

A coarse Lincolnshire voice, striving at an American accent and failing miserably, booms out over the loud speakers:

'On the yellow first game any line for two pounds nine eyes down all the eights eighty eight two fat ladies bless 'em . . . .

Anthony Clift

34

tin cars, a target, a robot and a packet of Kellogg's Special K. *Typographica* contains nothing comparable in graphic terms, or as direct in its acknowledgement of the phenomenon as IG member Reyner Banham's 'Who is this "Pop"?', published in *Motif* (winter 1962/3). Banham addresses Pop themes – mass media, air travel, science fiction, standardization, disposability – in slangy Pop prose, jazzed up by a glaring Pop-orange layout.[22] When Michael Middleton, writing in *Typographica*, belatedly noticed Pop, it was in a dismissive parenthesis: photography ought to have the makings, he writes, of a 'genuine popular art (as opposed to the hermetic fancies of Pop Art)'.[23]

There are, however, a handful of articles in *Typographica* which stray into Pop territory, or exhibit a sensibility with something in common. Anthony Clift's 'A rich man's guide to bingo', in 1963, accompanies an eye-witness account of a Cleethorpes bingo session with a folding inset constructed from photographs, bingo numbers and flowing proto-psychedelic orange and green Pop lettering to represent the bingo caller's voice. In a later issue, an article by Ann Gould on pattern books and clip art – which ranges in its references from Apollinaire and Malevich to Playboy bunnies and the Flintstones – also catches the idioms, rhythms and list-making relish of Pop. Colleagues and regular collaborators such as Alan Fletcher and Robert Brownjohn were much closer than Spencer in temperament and sympathy to the Pop codes and practices of 'swinging' London and they brought a distilled but aesthetically

Overleaf: *Typographica*, NS no. 10, December 1964. Spread from 'Sex and typography' by Robert Brownjohn, showing stills from the opening titles of the James Bond film *From Russia with Love*. Type was projected on to the model's moving body.

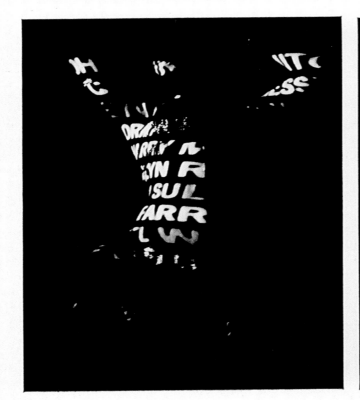

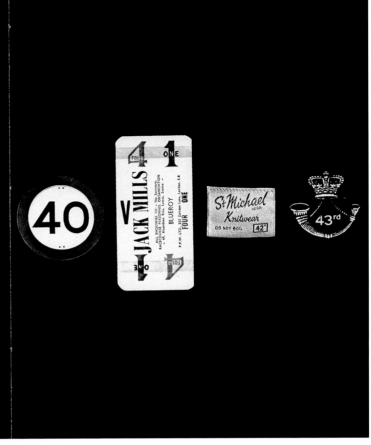

Technique 3.1 Photograph with shadow

3.4 Silhouette

3.7 With background

3.2 Photograph without shadow

3.5 Negative

3.8 Free drawing

3.3 Line

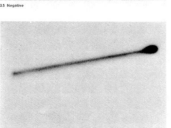

3.6 Out of focus

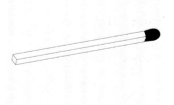

3.9 Mechanical drawing

Above: Bob Gill, Alan
Fletcher and Colin Forbes,
c.1962.

Opposite top:
Typographica, NS no. 15,
June 1967. Spread from
'Objects count' by
Crosby/Fletcher/Forbes.
Opposite bottom:
Typographica, NS no. 14,
December 1966. Spread
from 'A book of matches'
by Crosby/Fletcher/Forbes.
Both projects were
originally published by
the designers as self-
promotional A4 booklets.

arresting form of Pop to his pages. Brownjohn's *From Russia
with Love* film titles – slides of type projected on to a dancer's
body to form undulating light patterns – combine a Pop response
to popular culture with an experimental treatment of letterforms
(derived from Brownjohn's teacher, Moholy-Nagy, who
proposed projecting advertisements on to clouds at night) of
particular interest to Spencer, who had also taken pictures
of Brownjohn at work on the *Goldfinger* titles. In June 1967, in
the penultimate issue, 'Objects count' by Crosby/Fletcher/Forbes
is a found-object number game, in a direct line of descent
from Brownjohn's 'Street level' appropriations, which effects
a knowing graphic transmutation of ordinary artefacts and
cast-offs – road signs, a camera, a crossword puzzle, a Seven-up
can – into the conceptual source material of Pop graphic design.

Much closer to Spencer's concerns than British or American
Pop was the European avant-garde's investigation of the
letterform exemplified by Hamilton's article on Diter Rot's
books. As early as *Typographica*'s second issue, Spencer had
published an article on the ornamental lettering of Imre Reiner,
which indicated, according to his introduction, 'new paths
of expression'. W. J. Strachan's article in the sixth issue on
French artists working with writers' texts was titled 'The
liberation of the letter' and this was injected with some local
meaning by the type experiments then being conducted by
students on Edward Wright's basic design course at the Central
School. Thirty years later, Spencer gave his anthology of 'major

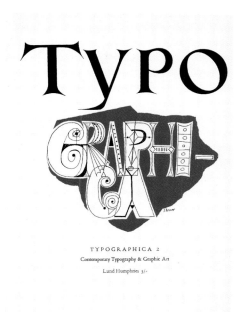

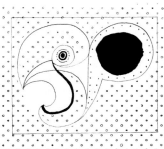

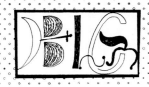

Above: *Typographica*, OS
no. 2, 1950. Design: Imre
Reiner.
Above right: *Typographica*,
OS no. 2. Spread from
'The ornamental lettering
of Imre Reiner'.

'TODAY MORE THAN EVER BEFORE, THE REALMS OF ART, POETRY, AND TYPOGRAPHY ARE MERGING IN THE TRADITION OF PICABIA AND LISSITZKY, WHO PRESENTED PICTORIAL AND LITERARY MESSAGES AS COMPLEMENTARY TO EACH OTHER. ARTISTS WHOSE WORK COMES INTO THIS CATEGORY DO NOT BELONG TO ANY SPECIFIC MOVEMENT AND THEIR WORK IS NOT PROGRAMMATIC.'

JASIA REICHARDT, 'TYPE IN ART', 1965

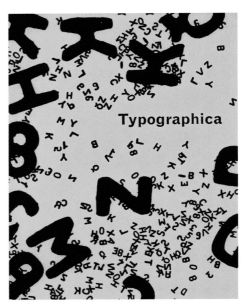

116

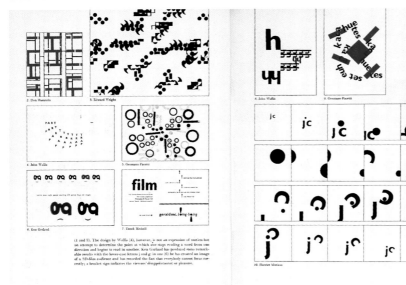

Above left: *Typographica*, OS no. 6, 1952. Opening spread from 'The Liberation of the letter' by W. J. Strachan.
Left: *Typographica*, OS no. 9, 1954. Spread from 'Pattern, sound, and motion', showing typographical experiments by Edward Wright and students at the Central School of Arts and Crafts, London, among them Ken Garland, Derek Birdsall, Germano Facetti and Harriet Morison.

Above: *Typographica*, NS no. 1, June 1960. Design: Spencer, using a photogram by Anne Hickmott.

typographic experiments of this century' first published in *Typographica*, the title *The Liberated Page*.[24] Not only were words and images breeding in the magazine's second series, but in the hands of typographically-minded artists words themselves were breeding new kinds of word-image.

Typographica, NS no. 8 is a key issue in the development of the magazine's interest in the liberation of letter and page, and demonstrates just how far it had strayed, by 1963, from the conventional concerns of a typography and design publication. Earlier in the year, the exhibition 'Schrift und Bild' ('Writing and art'), had moved from the Stedelijk Museum, Amsterdam to the Staatliche Kunsthalle, Baden-Baden, and Spencer included a review by Nicolete Gray in the issue. An ambitious and important survey, 'Schrift und Bild' featured among its 427 paintings, collages, photomontages and printed pieces examples by Braque, Klee, Schwitters, Léger, Apollinaire, Marinetti, Lissitzky, Werkman and Alcopley.[25] Of particular interest to Gray was the newer work:

> Apart from the making, crumpling, juxtaposing of textures, it showed the traces of words and writing, all the trail of association, known, half known, and lost, that one consciously associates more with poetry than visual art, it showed graphic movement pursued as an end, the artist 'writing' sign after sign, and the signs moving, changing, coming to life . . .[26]

One of the new artists singled out by Gray, Josua Reichert (b. 1937), was also included in the issue, in an article by the writer and exhibition organizer Jasia Reichardt. Reichert, a 'printer-

Right: *Typographica*, NS no. 8, December 1963. Spreads from 'Josua Reichert: typography as visual poetry' by Jasia Reichardt.

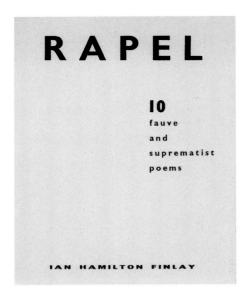

designer-artist' based in Munich, was influenced by H. N. Werkman's treatment of typography as material for making visual poetry. Some of Reichert's compositions were produced on an antiquated press; others were printed by spreading huge sheets of paper on the floor and standing on old wooden letters originally used for making posters. In Reichert's homage to Werkman's 1920s review *The Next Call*, the overprinting of letters is so severe that their individual outlines are obliterated, an acknowledgement by Reichert – suggests Reichardt – that the 'exchanges' of meaning Werkman hoped to effect in his review were not verbal in essence.

At the opposite end of the issue, balanced against Reichert, is a second excursion into the *terra incognita* of visual poetry, undertaken by dom Sylvester Houédard (1924–92) – Benedictine monk, scholar and creator of wordless 'typestracts' using an Olivetti typewriter. Houédard's extraordinary essay on concrete poetry and Ian Hamilton Finlay (b. 1925), Scottish 'poetoypographer', as Houédard describes the artist, is written in an orthographically peculiar and poetically compressed prose style that suggestively demonstrates its subjects' desire to contract and constrict language into constructive new forms of 'semantic economy':

> Words: hard & lovely as diamonds demand to be seen, freed in space; words are wild, sentences tame them. Every word an abstract painting, read quickly in a phrase words get lost: in concrete, eye sees words as objects that release sound/thought echoes in reader . . . concrete poems

118

Top: *Rapel* by Ian Hamilton Finlay, 1963, 265 × 212 mm. Folder containing poems on separate sheets. Publisher: Wild Hawthorn Press.
Above: *Typographica*, NS no. 8, December 1963. Spread from 'Concrete poetry & Ian Hamilton Finlay' by dom Sylvester Houédard. *The Formal Poem*, left, is reproduced from *Rapel*.

Above right: Finlay's manuscript for the *Notice Poem* as supplied to Spencer, with pencil request for an 'ornamental border', 216 × 165 mm.

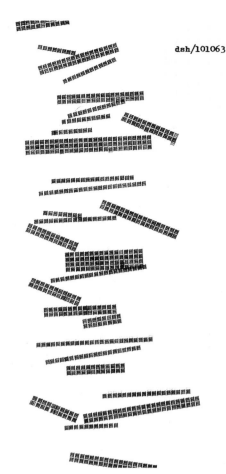

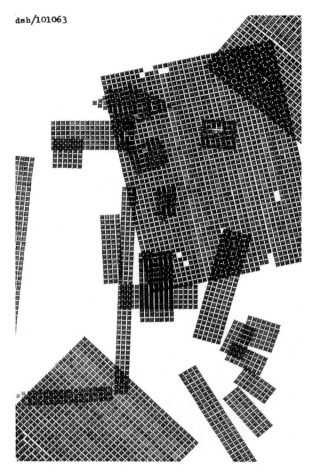

119

Above and above right:
'Typestracts' by dom
Sylvester Houédard, based
on the letter 'm', created
with an Olivetti manual
typewriter and mailed
to Spencer, 1963, each
203 × 127 mm.
Right: Letter to the Spencers
from Houédard, 1960s (date
unknown), 329 × 204 mm.
Below: dom Sylvester
Houédard, monk and
concrete poet, 1963.

prinknash abbey
gloucester

my dear h ERBErt and

marianne

it seems a great age

since i heard from you

& since i last wrote to you

& one got so much pleasure from yr **penrose**

& the last **typographica**

filled w/ lovely things by jasia & stefan's anatol

you must put them all in a vast automobile

& drive them down again

i ought to make a collection of typestracts

but they get dispersed to people so quickly

on loan often but thats just as bad

theres talk of expos in oxford cambridge & NY

plus something in paris

perhaps jasia might think of one in ica

i'm told **link** has just reproduced one

no — two

& made absolute messes

i must to have one **one** reproduced well in my lifetime

wld be quite an experience

tho admittedly i do aim at a certain degree

of unreproducibility

perhaps jn willet will do the **dop**i did for **tls** decently

a pity yr idea of having some in typographica hasnt come off

did ed wright show you the alfabet i did him?

i used a version for the title of one i did for jasia

a very nice (& very young)(30-ish) tibetan abbot (& reincarnation)

trungpa tulku rimpoche

came down to see us the other day

he is up at oxford (or rather in oxford)

looking at **l'ecriture** in **l'encyclopedie essentielle**

he was pleased to see a tibetan text — w/ he sd musical notation

he sang a bit

i thought then that you hadnt had exactly **much** on tibetan graphics

theres a lot one wld like to know abt the **tibetan book**

the

IMAGES AND WORDS ARE BREEDING

'CONCRETE POETRY BEGINS BY BEING AWARE OF GRAPHIC SPACE AS ITS STRUCTURAL
AGENT... A PRINTED CONCRETE POEM IS AMBIGUOUSLY BOTH TYPOGRAPHIC–POETRY
AND POETIC–TYPOGRAPHY – NOT JUST *A* POEM IN *THIS* LAYOUT, BUT A POEM THAT
IS ITS OWN TYPE ARRANGEMENT. HENCE MANY TYPE LAYOUTS ARE POEMS.'

DOM SYLVESTER HOUÉDARD, 'CONCRETE POETRY & IAN HAMILTON FINLAY', 1963

**Above: Ian Hamilton Finlay,
concrete poet, early 1960s.
Right: *Between Poetry
and Painting* catalogue
for an exhibition at the
Institute of Contemporary
Arts, London, in October
to November 1965,
201 × 204 mm.
Design: James Meller.**

just ARE: have no outside reference; they are objects like TOYS & TOOLS (toys can be tools), jewel-like concrete things-in-them-selves . . .[27]

In a letter to Spencer, written while he was working on the article, Houédard enthused about the typographic notebook by Brownjohn, Chermayeff and Geismar published in *Typographica*, NS no. 6: '*who* was the genetic genius that genesised watching words move (or whatever – I loaned mine to guernsey uncle) in last typogggggg?' For Houédard, these typographic explorations by designers who would go on to establish themselves in New York and London as leading professionals were 'superb concrete poems'.[28] Spencer's *Typographica* layout lends additional weight to the comparison by surrounding poems such as *S.O.S* and *The Practice* – like the economical word animations in *Watching words move* – with fields of white space.

In the mid-1960s, the international concrete poetry movement, which had its geographically confused origins in the 1950s, drew increasing attention in Britain.[29] For its exponents and critics, concrete poetry was seen – as Houédard expresses it in *Typographica* – as a 'reincarnation of pre-WW/1 creativities in the post-WW/2 world'. Writing about 'Type in art' for Spencer's *Penrose Annual*, Jasia Reichardt ends a historical survey which includes the usual sources – Apollinaire, Marinetti, Lewis Carroll's 'The Mouse's Tale' – with examples of concrete poems by Diter Rot, Ferdinand Kriwet, Ian Hamilton Finlay, John Furnival, and Houédard.[30] In 1965, her essay was reprinted in the catalogue for 'Between Poetry and Painting', an international survey of visual poetry organized by Reichardt and held at London's Institute of Contemporary Arts. Among the 48 participants were Finlay, Houédard, Furnival, Edwin Morgan, Hansjörg Mayer and Josua Reichert. The underlying basis, writes Reichardt, for this attempt to document a 'hybrid form of expression' that eludes a single accurate definition is the 'idea that the poet is a designer (in its widest context) of language' and that this applies equally to semiotic, semantic, concrete, visual, typewriter, phonetic, machine and kinetic poetry.[31]

Against this background of interest in the visual arts community, the later issues of *Typographica* return with uncompromising fascination to the liberation of the letter. A profile of Massin in NS no. 11 is prefaced by two reproductions, including one by Kriwet, from a series of *Poem/Prints* published by Finlay's Wild Hawthorn Press. The following issue features a folded sheet from Diter Rot's book-in-fragments for the Copley Foundation in Chicago, consisting of 112 folded and unfolded sheets of different sizes, fixed to a cardboard cover by a single staple.[32] A demanding article in NS no. 13 on the austere serial patterns of Wolfgang Schmidt (1929–95), a Frankfurt graphic artist inspired by the pictures of Max Bill, does not reveal until its final sentence that Schmidt has also undertaken commercial projects, including the visual communications for the new Frankfurt underground.

As with photography and the new typography, Spencer's examination of the contemporary liberated word was

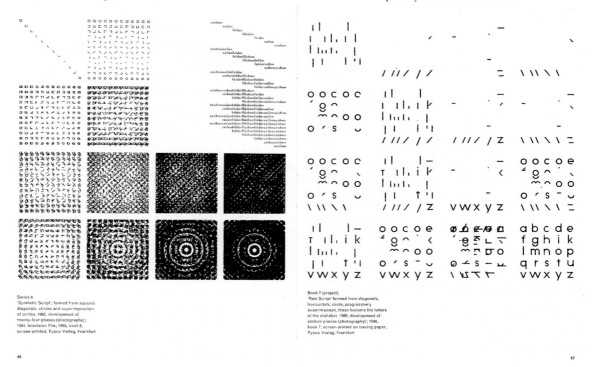

Typographica, NS no. 13, June 1966. Spread from 'Aesthetic pattern programme' by Eckhard Neumann. Serial patterns, created within a strict objective system, by the graphic artist Wolfgang Schmidt.

Series 6
'Synthetic Script', formed from squares diagonals, circles and superimposition of circles. 1962, development of twenty-four phases (photography); 1964, television film; 1965, book 6, screen-printed. Typos Verlag, Frankfurt

Book 7 (project)
'Real Script' formed from diagonals, horizontals, circle, progressively superimposed, these become the letters of the alphabet. 1965, development of sixteen phases (photography); 1966, book 7, screen-printed on tracing paper, Typos Verlag, Frankfurt

121

I Semantic Development 2

The free from complexity
                or intricacy,
                        direct,
                        clear
arrangement of the ultimate units of speech in sentences
builds solid figures with twelve five-angled faces
                common
                    to
                    a
            common mineral of a pale
                    fool's-gold colour
                    and brilliant
                        metallic
                        lustre

an arrangement like : This portion of space-time is ; I,
                that portion of space-time is : there,
                this & that have a common part

an arrangement like : You transfer
                this something
                good or bad
            material or non-material
whether for nothing or in exchange for something else
from your own possession
                control
            to that of his

an arrangement like : Person under arrest and in custody,
                charged with a crime
                    or offence
            who are standing now
            at the railing in this court of law
            at the railing which separates from the
                rest of the hall
                the part
                where we, judges, sit,
                where you, persons under arrest and
                    in custody, charged with

Left: Page from a prospectus
for *Semantic Sonata No. 2*
by Stefan Themerson, 1950,
219 × 142 mm. Design and
printing: Anthony Froshaug.

Below: *The Visible Word*
by Spencer, 1968, 299 ×
420 mm. A paper by Spencer
on printers and designers,
left, is rearranged by
Themerson according to
the principles of internal
vertical justification, right.
Publisher: Royal College
of Art, London.

The visible word: Some results of research

This page from a booklet presented to
members of the Double Crown Club, below,
has been rearranged, opposite, by Stefan
Themerson according to the principles of
IVJ, or internal vertical justification.

Printers and designers

Printers and designers

It is a well-worn platitude that the purpose of the printed word is to be read. This is a
gross understatement. The purpose of all printing, whether of words or of pictures, is
to communicate – ideas, information, instructions or emotions. The printed message
should be not merely read but understood. Often its purpose is to spark off ideas or
activities.
Society will, in the long run, use printing only for those tasks which printing can fulfil
more effectively, reliably and economically than other competing mediums of
communication.
The present decade is a fascinating and exciting period in printing and publishing. A
wide range of technical developments is waiting to be exploited by imaginative printers,
designers and authors and bold publishers willing to adopt energetic (and not
necessarily conventional) methods of selling and distributing their products. In a
century so packed with important developments in science and technology and man's
political ideas and social outlook, the book as a tool of civilization has an invaluable
function to perform. If all the achievements of scientists, scholars and technologists
in this century are not suddenly to collapse like a house of cards, specialists in one
field must somehow keep in touch with the thoughts and aims and achievements of
other men working in others. Television, films, radio all have an important part to
play in answering this challenge. But the book still has unique advantages: it is
passive; it is permanent; it is portable. The owner of a book can take what it has to
offer wherever and whenever he wishes – and at his own pace. He can consult several
books on the same subject at the same time, and so try to arrive at a balanced
personal judgment. No other method of communication offers all these advantages.
And what is true of the book is equally true of many other kinds of printing.
But while it is true that for many purposes the printed word has advantages over other

40

It is a well-worn platitude that the purpose of the printed word is to be read.
                This is a gross understatement.
The purpose of all printing, whether of words
                            or of pictures,
        is to communicate – ideas,
                        information,
                        instructions
                        or emotions.
The printed message should be not merely read
                            but understood;
        its purpose is to spark off ideas
                        or activities.

Society will, in
            the
            long
            run,
        use printing only for those tasks
                which printing can fulfil more effectively,
                            reliably
                        & economically
                than other competing mediums
                                    of
                                communi-
                                cation.

The present decade is a fascinating
                & exciting period in printing
                            & publishing.

A wide range of technical developments
        is waiting to be exploited by imaginative printers,
                            designers
                            & authors
                        & bold publishers willing to adopt
                            energetic
                            (and not necessarily conventional)
                            methods of selling
                                & distributing their
                                    products.

In a century so packed with important developments in science
                            & technology
                        & man's political ideas
                            & social outlook,
the book as a tool of civilization has an invaluable function to perform.

If all the achievements of scientists,
                        scholars
                    & technologists in this century
        are not suddenly to collapse like a house of cards,
specialists in one field must
                somehow
                keep in touch with the thoughts
                        & aims
                    & achievements of other men
                            working in others.

Television,
        films,
        radio all have an important part to play in answering this challenge.
But
    the book still has unique advantages: it is passive;
                                it is permanent;
                                it is portable.

or they can start an illicit liaison, so intimately integrated that one doesn't know any
more who is the bride and who is the bridegroom:

Left: *pour Irène Lagut (1917)*
Below: *Poèmes Retrouvés*
(Œuvres Poétiques, nrf, Pléiade)

What is it that makes us so excited when we see these two species of the same genus
going to bed together and uniting, which they often do with more grace than may be
found in a sanctified wedlock, more passion than is legislated for, and more
inventiveness than the aesthetic patent offices can willingly swallow?
Who is that terrible infant in our minds who rubs his dirty hands lustfully when some
innocent thoughts on some innocent things, such as:

a coffin   a mirror   a bird   a broken heart   a war

are put into words arranged into a sort of visual *haiku*, or is it a *Valentine*?
Is he drawn to them so much because they are seldom too serious to smile, even if
sadly?

Signs, symbols, archetypes; swallows, doves, ministers plenipotentiary; badges,
images, pictures. Words.
They all represent something. But
do they need to resemble the thing they represent?
is it an awful crime if they
Is it wrong that the word 'long' is spelled with four letters and therefore is shorter than
the five-letter word 'short'?
To create the impression of *longueur*, a lyric writer will repeat the short word 'long'
twice. He will make us sing:
Good-bye Piccadilly, Farewell Leicester Square;
It's a long, long way to Tipperary,
but my heart's right there!
Should the printer use extended type to print the word 'long', and condense his faces
for 'short'?
Should a sign for 'square' be squ/are, and
a sign for 'red' be red, and
a sign for 'wet' be wet?
Is the sign 'H₂O' truer when it is printed in *aquarella* ink, and
the sign for our purification / initiation clearer
when it is sprinkled with water, or bloodied with circumcision?
How much Infinity is there in '∞'?
How much Summer in just one lonely swallow?
How much Respect in a salute?
How much Fatherland in an ambassador?
How much Deity in a holy picture?
&
How much of a Table in a 'table'?

There is a difference between a table and a 'table'.
A table has four legs; a 'table' has five letters.
This typographical device ' ' & " " is used by linguistic philosophers to make clear
whether they mean a particular thing (a table) or the word that designates it (a 'table').
It sounds childishly simple, but . . . But what shall we do with Apollinaire's 'tables'?
They are not tables (one cannot sit at them), they are 'tables'. And yet, they have both
'legs' *and* letters. One has four 'legs' and 103 letters. The other has one 'leg' and 137
letters. They have letters, not 'letters' (you *can* read them); but they have 'legs', not
legs (you can't break them).

5

123

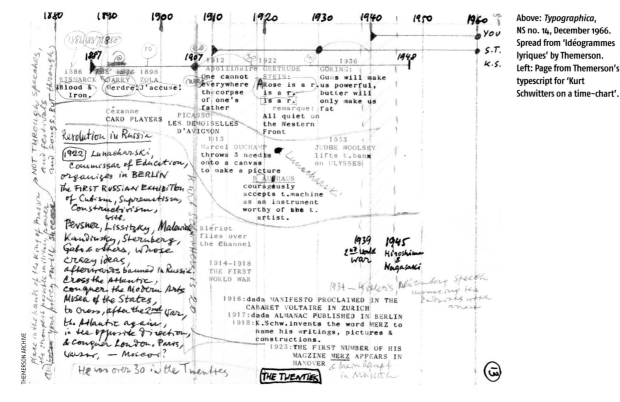

Above: *Typographica*,
NS no. 14, December 1966.
Spread from 'Idéogrammes
lyriques' by Themerson.
Left: Page from Themerson's
typescript for 'Kurt
Schwitters on a time-chart'.

Overleaf: *Typographica*,
NS no. 16, December 1967.
Spread from 'Kurt
Schwitters on a time-chart' by Themerson.

1880 1890 1900 1910 1920 1930 1940 1950 1960

I have just come back from Cambridge, where I was asked to address a Society of Arts on Kurt Schwitters in England. The average age of the audience was about 20. Consequently, I learnt more from them than they did from me. What I learnt I will tell you later. One of my tasks was to make those 20-year-old men and women see that the objects they liked or disliked (such objects as Schwitters' collages) were produced in a world quite larger than theirs, in a world in which clocks turn much more quickly than do those embedded in the old walls of the colleges. Their minds lived in the specially cultivated quiescent isolation of the university green lawns. The objects they wanted to know whether to like or dislike came to them from a different context. They were produced in a world which changes with each turn of its clocks.

I drew a time-chart on the blackboard:

When Who Was Twenty

Just to see Who lived When. No, not when who was born, or who died when. I thought it would be much more interesting to see

Twenty is probably the time when the retina of our eye becomes tattooed with the picture of reference points from which we later measure different historical perspectives. Till we are 20, we depend on other people. They are therefore responsible for the World. At about 20, more and more people begin to depend on us. We are therefore responsible for the world. 'Now', I said, 'let us see where we were 20. You (the audience), I, whor. you see in the flesh, and Kurt Schwitters on whom I am asked to address you.' Whereupon I drew three horizontal lines on the time-chart, and the lines terrified them. Secure and detached as they felt in their black gowns (which, incidentally, they kept tucked away under their arms), they suddenly realized that they were not set apart, not exempt, they suddenly saw themselves involved. Not 'committed', just involved in the inescapable machinery of time that is swallowed up by shifting human live

Queen Victoria was 20 three inches from the edge of this page

Victoria.

Kurt Schwitters was 20 in 1907

when Schwitters was   20
Bertrand Russell was   35
Churchill & Chesterton were   33
Adenauer & Marinetti were   31
Stalin & Einstein were   28
Hitler was   18
Eisenhauer & De Gaulle were   17
Macmillan & Khrushchev were   13
Mr Gaitskell was   1

I was 20 in 1930

Cambridge students were 20 in 1960

S.T.

K.S.

This dotted line is for you, gentle reader. Where were you 20 ?

Prices of Post-Impressionists: 1927-60
(based on information from 'Observer' 18.11.62)

£90,000
£80,000
£70,000
£60,000
£50,000
£40,000
£30,000
£20,000
£10,000
£00,000

ART AS AN INVESTMENT

Cézanne

Van Gogh

Gauguin

Somewhere here (1886) BISMARCK says: **'Blood and Iron!'**

'Place in the hands of the King of Prussia the strongest possible military power and your policy will succeed not through speeches and festivals and songs, but through Blood and Iron

---

Somewhere here JARRY says: **'Merdre!'**

and ZOLA: **'J'accuse!'**

Here CEZANNE paints his **CARD PLAYERS**

Somewhere here (1912) APOLLINAIRE says: **'One cannot carry everywhere the corpse of one's father.'**

Here MARCEL DUCHAMP throws **3 needles** on to a canvas to make a picture;

*1913

& PICASSO his **DEMOISELLES D'AVIGNON** *

& GERTRUDE STEIN: **'A rose is a rose is a rose.'**

Somewhere here REMARQUE writes: **'All quiet on the Western Front'.**

THE BAUHAUS **'courageously accepts the machine as an instrument worthy of an artist.'**

& GÖRING. (1936) **'Guns will make us powerful, butter will only make us fat!.'**

*1933

and JUDGE WOOLSEY lifts the ban on **ULYSSES.**

Typographica 16

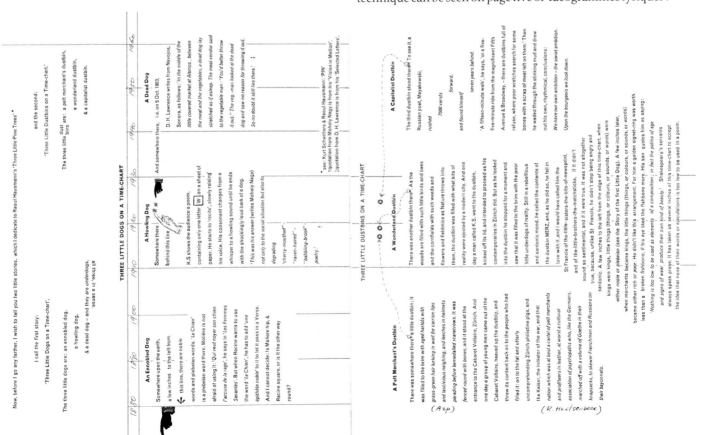

Above: *Typographica*, NS no. 16, December 1967. Design: Spencer, using a letter to the Themersons from Kurt Schwitters.
Below and opposite: *Typographica*, NS no. 16. Consecutive spreads from 'Kurt Schwitters on a time-chart' by Stefan Themerson.

accompanied by historical investigations into the genre's precursors. In NS no. 15, Paul Vincent and regular *Typographica* collaborator Edward Wright analyse the achievement of the Flemish poetic innovator Paul van Ostaijen (1896–1928), author in 1921 of the 153-page *Bezette Stad* ('Occupied city') in which Wright identifies nine distinct graphic techniques: 'the graphic pattern', he suggests, 'is a true notation of the sound, sense and rhythm' of the Flemish language. Spencer devoted 19 pages of the issue to the reappraisal of a poet virtually unknown at that point in the English-speaking world.

In 'Idéogrammes lyriques' in NS no. 14, Stefan Themerson returns to the more familiar figure of Apollinaire – always among the first to be cited in any consideration of visual poetry – to discover to what extent the poet himself was involved in the typography and printing of *calligrammes* such as 'Il pleut'. Themerson's article is notable for the care with which its layout brings together his commentary – like Houédard's, his prose style is idiosyncratic – and the manuscripts and typeset poems, which are allowed to break into the text at the point where they are discussed, encouraging the reader to move fluidly from one to the other. The compositional method treats the visual image with something of the semantic logic seen in Themerson's theory of 'internal vertical justification' in which lines of normally continuous prose are broken into shorter units and aligned vertically according to their verbal sense; a limited use of the technique can be seen on page five of 'Idéogrammes lyriques'.

A year earlier, in *The Penrose Annual*, Spencer had published a version of his own paper, 'Printers and designers' (1963), reinterpreted by Themerson as an example of internal vertical justification.[33] In perhaps the most suggestive moment of implied fusion in Spencer's parallel researches into the legible and liberated page, he later reprinted the two versions side by side in *The Visible Word*.[34]

Typographica ends with the most radical contribution, in typographic and structural terms, ever published in its pages. The final article of the final issue, in December 1967, is an inquiry by Stefan Themerson into the contemporary meaning of Kurt Schwitters' collage aesthetic, cast in the form of a 'time-chart' which flows horizontally from page to page, turning each spread into a single visual unit.[35] Part essay, part autobiographical reminiscence, part diagram and part collage, the article defies conventional publishing categories. Themerson is engaged, with effortless wit and exceptional imagination, in a new form of visual writing made possible by the history of typographic experimentation featured in so many issues of *Typographica*. In 'Kurt Schwitters on a time-chart', design and writing can no longer be separated; they have fused to become a composite process. Typography has ceased to be a quiescent channel for orderly, sequential argument and become an active visual medium for the living complexity of thought. In the process, the bureaucratic conventions of post-war 'new typography', observed throughout the second series in *Typographica*'s own typography, are called into question and abandoned. The seamless professionalism of the page is breached by handwritten annotations and skewed by uneven lines of type and stray text running at angles. Multiple text paths and the fragmented nature of the page encourage readers to break with conventional patterns of reading and enter at any point. In this way, Themerson's time-chart prefigures the non-linear structures of the electronic book and interactive multimedia.

In his final editorial, Spencer reflects on the 32 issues of *Typographica*. They span two decades, he notes,

> . . . in which the practice and the techniques of typography have changed dramatically, in which technical developments have released typography from the restrictions and the discipline imposed by metal type, and have allowed it to become increasingly visual and less linear, less linguistic. The frontiers between graphic design, photography, and typography have dissolved; the marriage of word and image has been consummated.[36]

There is a sense in Spencer's words (understandable after almost 19 years) that with the cessation of *Typographica*, the story of word and image, their marriage successfully 'consummated', has itself reached some kind of resolution. It is a measure of Spencer's achievement as editor-designer that more than 30 years later so much of this remarkably prophetic magazine remains pregnant with possibilities still not entirely explored.

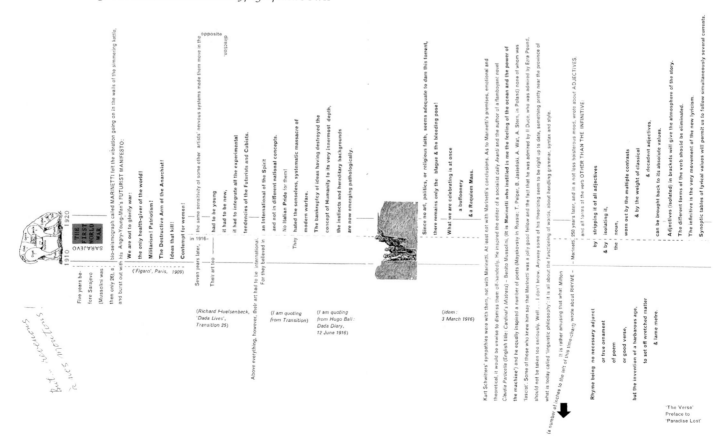

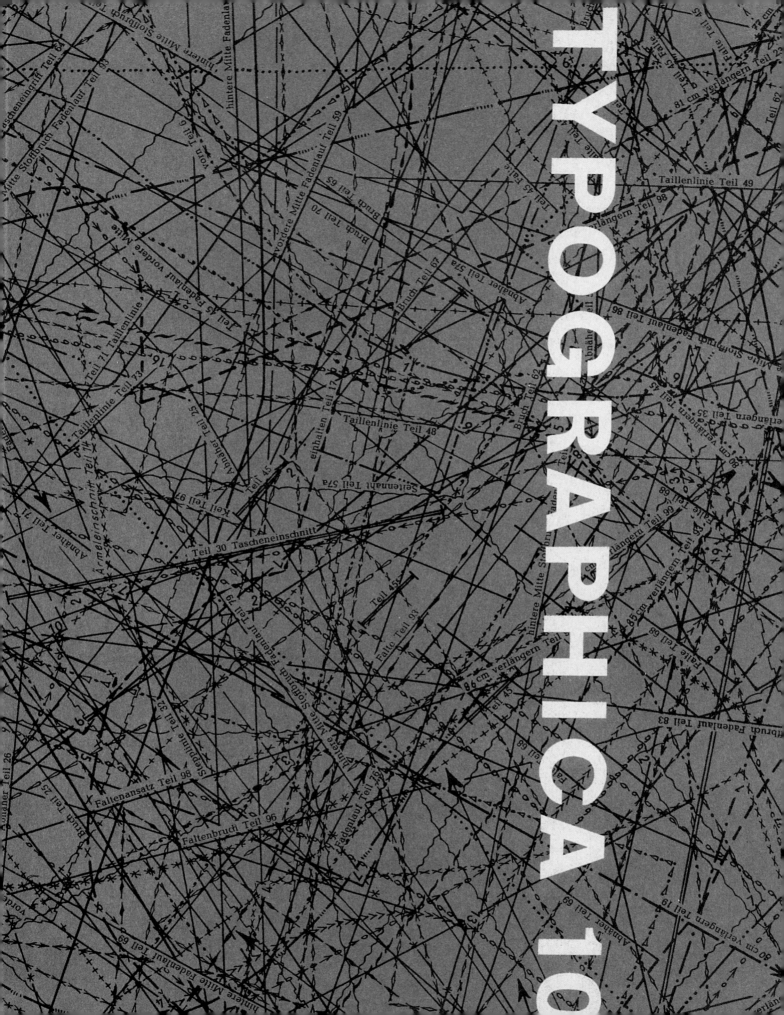

TYPO GRAPHICA 10

Articles published in *Typographica*

Old series nos. 1–16
310 x 236 mm except issue no. 2: 306 x 227 mm

No. 1 | 1949 | 24 pp.
Dr Konrad F. Bauer... *Magic and the art of writing*
Charles Hale... *The integration of photo and type*
John C. Tarr... *The use of space in typography*

No. 2 | 1950 | 38 pp.
R. S. Hutchings... *Copper-plate scripts*
Michael Middleton... *Political typography*
Imre Reiner... *The ornamental lettering of Imre Reiner*
Michael Alexander... *Visual aids*
Typographical review (examples by Anthony Froshaug, Ian
   Bradbery, Herbert Spencer, Max Bill)

No. 3 | 1950 | 38 pp.
Herbert Spencer... *Function & design in business printing*
Michael Middleton... *The possibilities of the photogram*
Alfred Lammer... *Central School experiments with photograms*
W. J. Strachan... *Modern French book illustration*
Ruari McLean, Christopher Foss... *Type review* (Miller and
   Richard's Egyptian; Profil – a new Swiss type)
Typographical design review (A-D Gallery, J. M. Beadle, RCA
   student, Alvin Lustig)

No. 4 | 1951 | 48 pp.
Geoffrey Dowding... *Type faces: a plea for rational terminology*
Toni del Renzio... *First principles and last hopes*
George Newman... *Music engraving*
W. J. Strachan... *Chastel's illustrations for 'Le Bestiaire'*
Typographical design review (RCA students' work)
Stuart F. Hayes... *Type review* (Studio: Amsterdam
   typefoundry)

No. 5 | 'Purpose and Pleasure' | 1952 | 40 pp.
Anthony Bell, Michael Middleton, Herbert Spencer...
   Introduction to the exhibition
Catalogue to the exhibition
Typographical design review (examples from the exhibits)
Herbert Simon... *Is there a 'new' style of typography?*
James Shand... *Illustration versus typography*
Paul Rand... *Modern typography in the modern world*
Max Bill... *Typography to-day*

Opposite: *Typographica*,
OS no. 10, 1955. Design:
Spencer, using a German
dressmaking pattern sheet.
Above: OS no. 2,
frontispiece. Lithograph
by Robert Adams.

130

Above: OS no. 6.
Design: Spencer.
Below: OS no. 8, back cover.
Typographical experiments
by Ken Garland.
Bottom: OS no. 11.
Design: Spencer.

No. 13 | 1957 | 40 pp.
Germano Facetti ... *French book clubs*
Stuart F. Hayes ... *Factors in the choice of type faces* (book review)
Patricia Davey ... *Locomotive lettering*
Edward Wright ... *The arrow in the road*
Alain Bosquet ... *The illustrations of Avigdor Arikha*
Books for typographers (list of books published in 1955 and 1956)

No. 14 | 1958 | 40 pp.
Herbert Spencer ... *The publications of Gaberbocchus Press*
Walter Plata ... *Two German presses*
Bibliography of the Grillen-Presse
Bibliography of the Eggebrecht-Presse
Books for typographers (list of books published in 1957)
Sandberg's Experimenta Typographica
Alan Fern ... *Old-fashioned types and new-fangled typography*

No. 15 | 1958 | 40 pp.
Walter Tracy ... *Telephone directories*
Ken Garland ... *Lunch-hour photograms*
Walter Plata ... *Büchergilde Gutenberg*
The Crawford Gallery presents ...
G. W. Ovink ... *Dutch chocolate letters*

No. 16 | 1959 | 44 pp.
Henri Friedlaender ... *Modern Hebrew typefaces*
Prof. G. van den Bergh ... *Capitals, twin- and multi-print* (inset red/green paper spectacles)
Camilla Gray ... *El Lissitzky: typographer*
Paul Hogarth ... *A History of Book Illustration* (book review)

New series nos. 1–16
272 × 210 mm

No. 1 | June 1960 | 64 pp.
Charles Hasler ... *Britain's Royal Arms*
Adam Johann ... *Five Polish photographers*
Penuel Peter Kahanne ... *Yosl Bergner's drawings to Kafka*
Alan Bartram ... *The work of Franco Grignani*
Henri Friedlaender ... *The history of numerals*
Photograms by Anne Hickmott
Herbert Spencer ... *Farewell to Trajan* (review of *Lettering on Buildings* by Nicolete Gray)

No. 2 | December 1960 | 60 pp.
B. Majorick ... *de Jong, Hilversum*
BCG (Brownjohn, Chermayeff and Geismar)
Sylvio Samama ... *The books of Abram Krol*
Edward Wright ... *'The Green Box'* (book review, with 4 pp. inset)
Antonio Boggeri ... *Max Huber in Italy*
A humanized alphabet (Stefan Themerson's initials from *Exercises in Style*)

No. 3 | June 1961 | 76 pp.
Ken Garland ... *Typophoto*
Richard Hamilton ... *The books of Diter Rot* (fold-out pages)
National Zeitung (fold-out pages)
Herbert Spencer ... *The drawings of Alcopley*
Camilla Gray ... *From painting to photography: experiments of the 1920s*

Below: OS no. 16, back cover.
Design: Franco Grignani.
Bottom: NS no. 1, front cover (under wrapper).
Example of the Royal Arms.

131

132

Top: NS no. 5, front cover
(under wrapper).
Design: Spencer.
Above: NS no. 7, back cover.
Design: Spencer.

No. 11 | June 1965 | 52 pp.
Camilla Gray … *Alexander Rodchenko: a Constructivist designer*
Nicolete Gray … *The inscriptional work of Eric Gill* (book review)
Poem/Prints
Germano Facetti … *Massin*
Eckhard Neumann … *Herbert Bayer's photographic experiments*
John Berger … *Words and images*
John Berger … *At Remaurian* (inset 38 pp. booklet)

No. 12 | December 1965 | 76 pp.
James Mosley … *The nymph and the grot: the revival of the sanserif letter*
Barbara Jones … *Fishing figures*
Aloisio Magalhães … *The living symbol*
Ann Gould … *Art on the assembly line*
Diter Rot (book review, with folding inset)
Edward Wright … *Emphatic fist, informative arrow*
K. P. Mayer … *The arrow in China*

No. 13 | June 1966 | 62 pp.
Frederick Burgess … *Tombstone lettering on slate*
Henry Steiner … *Hong Kong signs*
Eckhard Neumann … *Aesthetic pattern programmes*
Ernst Hoch and Maurice Goldring … *Type size: a system of dimensional references*
James Sutton … *Of the Just Shaping of Letters* (book review)

No. 14 | December 1966 | 58 pp.
Stefan Themerson … *Idéogrammes lyriques*
Crosby/Fletcher/Forbes … *A book of matches*
Ann Gould … *Protest by design*

133

No. 15 | June 1967 | 56 pp.
Edward Wright … *Paul van Ostaijen*
Paul Vincent … *Paul van Ostaijen: Lyric poetry – instructions for use*
Crosby/Fletcher/Forbes … *Objects count*
Alan Bartram … *Spanish street lettering*

No. 16 | December 1967 | 52 pp.
Herbert Spencer … *Typographica 1949–67*
Eckhard Neumann … *John Heartfield*
Berjouhi Barsamian Bowler … *The word as ikon*
Stefan Themerson … *Kurt Schwitters on a time-chart*

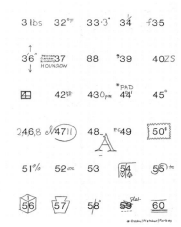

Top: NS no.11, front cover
(under wrapper). Page
from *La Cantatrice Chauve*
designed by Massin.
Centre: NS no. 14, front
cover (under wrapper).
Engraving by William Blake.
Above: NS no. 15, back
cover. Design:
Crosby/Fletcher/Forbes.

Notes

1. New formations

1. Middleton, M., 'Sunday photographers', *Typographica*, NS no. 9, June 1964, p. 35. The quotation is also used by Spencer in *Pioneers of Modern Typography*, p. 5. It is taken from 'A new instrument of vision', 1932, by Moholy-Nagy, reprinted, in a slightly different translation, in Kostelanetz, R., 1970, p. 54.

2. See McLean, R., 1992, p. 69, and Kinross, R., 1987, p. 56, 1990, p. 528 and 1992, p. 118.

3. See, for instance, Sewell, J., 1954, and Forbes, C., 1960. Forbes, a former assistant of Spencer, and later a Pentagram partner, reports his disappointment that *Typographica*, NS no. 1, is 'filled with articles that are only of marginal interest to the typographer'.

4. Facetti, G., 1961, p. 79.

5. '… with typography I always thought one isn't doing one's own thing. [Or rather that] one is doing one's own thing, but linked to a very serious purpose, which is – if I can use this expression – forming a bridge between the writer and the reader. But that's now being disregarded. Much of what is currently being produced, although it's very clever and often quite pleasing in the aesthetic sense, perhaps, is more of a barrier than a bridge.' Interview with Spencer, 26 June 1995.

6. Kinross, R., 1992, p. 119.

7. Higgins, D., 1988, p. 30.

8. El Lissitzky, Theo van Doesburg, Kurt Schwitters, H. N. Werkman, Piet Zwart, Paul Schuitema, Alexander Rodchenko, Laszlo Moholy-Nagy, Herbert Bayer and Jan Tschichold. Of these, Spencer himself had previously written about Werkman, in *Typographica*, OS no. 11, 1955, and Zwart, in *Typographica*, NS no. 7, May 1963.

9. *Pioneers* continues to inspire fierce, even hyperbolic, loyalty: 'the only book on typography that ever meant anything. The only typography book that you really need.' Wood, G., 2000, p. 98.

10. For international surveys of the 'new typography' of the 1980s and 1990s, see Poynor, R. and Booth-Clibborn, E., 1991, and Poynor, R., 1996.

11. See Blauvelt, A., 1994, and Mermoz, G., 1994, p. 263. The typographic scene, Mermoz notes, 'has displayed a singular dogmatism when confronted with works conceived outside its ideological frame of reference'.

12. See Kinross, R., 1992, p. 119. Kinross identifies Spencer and Anthony Froshaug as pivotal figures in post-war British typography, but marks Spencer down for a lack of ideological engagement in his typographic advice – 'at least overtly. It was a typography for the mundane world of businessmen, in which simplifications of form meant efficiency and cost-saving, but without philosophical overtones.' Following publication of an article about *Typographica* in *Eye* (Poynor, R., 1999), Kinross wrote to the magazine to record his seduction by *Typographica* as a young 'aspiring designer'. Kinross, R., 1999.

13. Seago, A., 1995, p. 213.

14. Spencer, H., 1980, p. 6. See also Smith, B. H., 1975, p. 193, and Fletcher, A., 1981, p. 18.

15. Spencer, H., 1980, p. 6.

16. The term 'new traditionalism' is applied to French and Morgan by Kinross, R., 1985, p. 45: 'The new traditionalism was a peculiarly British phenomenon: the reforming movement in printing and typography that is associated with the names of Stanley Morison, Francis Meynell, Oliver Simon, and others. And the new traditionalism should be borne in mind as the reigning *enlightened* orthodoxy, against which new typography began to be adopted in Britain in the 1940s and 1950s.'

17. In the period under review, Spencer maintained studios at the following addresses: 1945–9, 90 Linden Gardens, London W2; 1949–51, 113 Harley Street, London W1; 1951–5, 44 Fulham Road, London SW3; 1955–67, 26 Blomfield Road, London W9; 1967–84, 30 Acacia Road, London NW8. After acquiring the Fulham Road studio, he continued to live in Harley Street until moving to Blomfield Road. Other than this four-year period, he has preferred to work from a studio and office at home.

18. See Wright, E., 1985, pp. 44–5. Wright reproduces part of the Anglo French Art Centre's 1946 programme.

19. Published in c. December 1947 by the Anglo French Art Centre, 29 Elm Tree Road, London NW8. The curriculum, 'under the direction of Herbert Spencer MSIA', consisted of 'Preliminary experiments' (composition, contrast, use of colour), 'Instruction' (typefaces, the point system, the em, spacing, paper sizes, printing signs and methods of correcting proofs), 'Experimental layouts' and 'Research and investigation'. In addition, lectures by specialists, and visits to printing works, papermills and blockmakers, were promised. Spencer's students included the illustrator Paul Hogarth.

20. Tschichold, J., 1937.

21. Fletcher, A., 1980, p. 18.

22. The back cover of *Typographica*, OS no. 6, 1952, is an abstract painting signed by Vera Spencer and an abstract design by her is used as a frontispiece in *Typographica*, OS no. 4, 1951. An example of her work is shown alongside paintings by Victor Pasmore, Robert Adams, Kenneth Martin, Anthony Hill and others in the article 'First principles and last hopes' by Toni del Renzio in *Typographica*, OS no. 4, 1951, p. 16.

23. 'Too damn English', *Alphabet and Image*, no. 6, January 1948, p. 1.

24. Editorial, *Alphabet and Image*, no. 1, spring 1946, p. 2.

134

25. Interview with Michael Middleton, 14 July 1997.

26. Spencer, H., 1980, p. 8.

27. *Signature* ceased publication in 1954.

28. Interview with Spencer, 26 June 1995.

29. Spencer, H., 1980, p. 8.

30. Interviews with Alan Fletcher, 19 May 1997; Ken Garland, 23 May 1997; Colin Forbes, 12 June 1997; Derek Birdsall, 9 July 1997; Philip Thompson, 23 July 1997. For an account of Froshaug's career, see Kinross, R., 2000.

31. See Smith, B. H., 1975, p. 196.

32. Spencer, H., 1950.

33. Spencer, H., 1952a, p. 37.

34. Hatch, P., 1952.

35. McLean, R., 1992, p. 184.

36. Spencer's commercial clients, up to the mid-1950s, included the film strips company Common Ground, the Contemporary Art Society, the pharmaceutical company Upjohn, architects Chamberlin Powell & Bon, and British Transport.

37. *Printing Review*, vol. 18 no. 4, winter 1953/4, p. 30. The exhibition of Spencer's typography and design was held at the Zwemmer Gallery, 26 Litchfield Street, London WC2, from 23 to 31 October 1953.

38. *The Griffith Graph*, August 1957, p. 2.

2. The designer as editor

1. Interview with Spencer, 10 August 1995.

2. *Typographica*, OS no. 16, 1959, p. 34. The message was repeated in an undated letter to subscribers headed 'Typographica: present and future'.

3. Interview with John Taylor, 12 June 1997.

4. *Typographica*, OS no. 7, 1953, p. 3.

5. *Typographica*, OS no. 7, 1953, p. 2.

6. *Typographica*, NS no. 5, June 1962, p. 72.

7. It is not possible to attribute precise, monthly publication dates to *Typographica*'s first series. After the first two issues, they are undated, even by year. The years of publication given in this book for nos. 3–16 have been supplied by Herbert Spencer and confirmed against the dates of contemporary reviews and other external and internal evidence.

8. *Typographica*, OS no. 16, 1959, p. 34.

9. Letter from Anthony Bell to Ken Garland, London, 23 November 1967. Bell is replying to Garland's letter of 21 November 1967, sent in appreciation to the directors of Lund Humphries following *Typographica*'s closure.

10. *Typographica*, NS no. 15, June 1967, p. 1.

11. Fletcher, A., 1981, p. 19.

12. Interview with Spencer, 10 August 1995.

13. For a full account (in German) of *Spirale*'s history and development, see Bucher, A., 1990. There is a brief discussion of *Spirale* in Moore, B. and Hendricks, J., 1985, p. 90.

14. By 1955, there were some 200 schools in Britain offering instruction (not always of great quality) in typography, according to Dowding, G., 'The training of typographers', *Typographica*, OS no. 10, 1955, p. 12. The leading schools were the Central School of Arts and Crafts, the London School of Printing and the Royal College of Art.

15. Interview with Spencer, 7 March 1996.

16. Interview with Ken Garland, 23 May 1997.

17. Interview with Alan Bartram, 4 July 1997.

18. Interview with Spencer, 10 August 1995.

19. In most magazines, editing and design are separate activities carried out by different individuals. Design, as the secondary task, is particularly dependent on the quality of the interaction between editor and designer. While trade magazines produced for designers also usually follow this pattern, design magazines are still the genre most likely to combine editor and designer in a single person. A much greater than usual emphasis on visual values often

results. See Owen, W., 1991, and VanderLans, R., and Licko, Z., 1993.

20. The second issue is anomalous. Spencer does not recall the details, but owing to what may have been an error in the imposition the printed issues had to be taken apart, reassembled and retrimmed as part of the re-binding process. As a result, the issue is slightly smaller in its dimensions than others in the first series. It also has a cover, in a heavier than usual weight of card, and a glassine wrapper rather than the usual printed wrapper.

21. The closest standard paper size to *Typographica* is A4 (297 x 210 mm), which became a common – and consequently rather lifeless – choice of size for magazines of all kinds. The second series of *Typographica* is similar to A4 in width, but 25 mm smaller in height. Spencer preferred the squarer, booklike shape.

22. See Spencer, H., 1952a, p. 72.

23. Interview with Spencer, 10 August 1995.

24. Duchamp, M., 1960.

25. Hamilton, R., 1959, unpaginated.

26. Letter from Ian Hamilton Finlay to Herbert Spencer, Edinburgh, 3 November 1963. In 1964, when the poem was published by Finlay's Wild Hawthorn Press, in a different typographic version, the border was restored, in blue. Finlay retained Spencer's black for the hoop and some of the red words, but rendered others in blue and a few in black. See *Artes Hispanicas/Hispanic Arts*, vol. 1 no. 3 & 4, winter/spring 1968, p. 209.

27. Kinross, R., 1984, pp. 89–90.

28. Interview with Spencer, 17 August 1995.

29. A comparable instance of this process of graphic assimilation occurred in an issue of the Californian design magazine *Emigre*, in an article about the Dutch magazine *Tijdschrift*. Unusually, the editor-designer explained his design strategy in a footnote. His arguments, quite different in spirit and intention from the

'objective' art historical approach, have much in common with Spencer's: 'when design artifacts are reproduced, something inevitably gets lost. No matter how perfect the reproductions can be, the look and feel, size, method of binding, page sequencing, etc., are all sacrificed. By taking apart the original work and reassembling it to specifically fit the page layouts and sequencing of *Emigre*, a new work was created…an integral part of this issue…' VanderLans, R., 1996, unpaginated.
30. Interview with Jasia Reichardt, 30 June 1997.

3. Assimilating the avant-garde

1. See Kinross, R., 1985, p. 45.
2. Tschichold, J., 1930a and 1930b.
3. Tschichold, J., 1937.
4. Tschichold, J., 1971, p. 249.
5. 'Bookshelf', *Typography*, no. 2, spring 1937, p. 22.
6. Harling, R., 1949, pp. 1–2.
7. Lewis, J. and Brinkley, J., 1954.
8. Editorial, *Typographica*, OS no. 1, 1949, p. 3.
9. Spencer, H., 1967c, p. 3.
10. Spencer is unable to recall who wrote the captions, but given his developing interests, it seems probable they are by him, rather than Tarr. None of the 'typographical experiments' are mentioned in Tarr's article.
11. 'Catalogue of the exhibition', *Typographica*, OS no. 5, 1952, pp. 5–24. The exhibition was held at Lund Humphries, 12 Bedford Square, London WC1, from 11 to 28 June 1952.
12. Bill, M., 'Typography to-day', *Typographica*, OS no. 5, 1952, p. 29. For an account of Bill's career and development as a typographer, see Fleischmann, G. *et al.*, 1999. The other contributors were: Herbert Simon, director of the Curwen Press, London; James Shand, director of the Shenval Press, London; Paul

Rand, designer and typographer, New York; and W. J. H. B. Sandberg, director of the Stedelijk Museum, Amsterdam, pp. 25–31.
13. Spencer, H., 1952a, p. 32.
14. Spencer, H., 1955a, p. 20.
15. For an alternative translation of Lissitzky's principles, see Bierut, M. *et al.*, 1999, p. 23.
16. The exhibition was held at Lund Humphries, 12 Bedford Square, London WC1, from 1 to 15 May 1963.
17. Spencer, H., 1967c, p. 2.
18. In the revised edition of *Pioneers of Modern Typography* (1982), Spencer's text on Werkman was replaced by a text written on the basis of new research by his daughter, Mafalda Spencer.
19. *Pioneers of Modern Typography* was one of the first surveys of this subject matter to appear in English and although it has been superseded in depth of historical and theoretical analysis by later studies – see, for instance, Drucker, J., 1994 – it has remained in print since the revised edition in 1982 as a standard introduction. It was, however, preceded by *Typographica* contributor Eckhard Neumann's *Functional Graphic Design in the 20's* (1967), which covers similar ground thematically, rather than by individual, but is less well illustrated.
20. Spencer, H., 1969, pp. 51, 64.
21. Mermoz, G., 1994, p. 276.
22. See, for instance, Marinetti's 'Destruction of syntax – Imagination without strings – Words-in-freedom 1913' in Apollonio, U., 1973, pp. 95–106. A section is reprinted in Bierut, M. *et al.*, 1999, pp. 6–11.
23. Spencer, H., 1969, p. 13.
24. Drucker, J., 1994, p. 10.
25. Drucker, J., 1994, p. 240.
26. Garland, K., 1960b, p. 9–10.
27. Fleming, A., 1961a, pp. 380–1. Extracts from 'In defence of typographic vulgarity', a talk given by Fleming, type director of Cooper & Beatty, to the Society of Typographic Designers

– on which this article is evidently based – were also published in *Design*, under the heading 'The tired typographer'. There are some minor changes of wording. See Fleming, A., 1961b, p. 65.
28. There is a change of wording between the two versions of the text. The edited transcript of the talk published in *Design* only mentions *Typographica*; the later text omits *Typographica* and mentions Wright and *Queen*.
29. *Typographica* contributor Alan Fletcher is the most notable example of American influence. After graduating from the Royal College of Art in 1956, he studied for an MFA at Yale University from 1956 to 1957, then stayed on in the US for another two years. He assisted Saul Bass, Paul Rand and Leo Lionni and worked in the design department at *Fortune* magazine. Fletcher's 'Letter from America', published in *Ark*, offers vivid impressions of the impact of the American scene on a young British designer. See Fletcher, A., 1957, pp. 36–9, and Myerson, J., 1996, pp. 256–8.

4. The camera as pen

1. Interview with Spencer, 28 March 1996.
2. Alfred Lammer wrote 'Central School experiments with photograms' in *Typographica*, OS no. 3, 1950, pp. 17–19.
3. See Bowman, J., 1962, pp. 9–32.
4. Spencer, H., 1967a. A second collection of 32 pictures, *Without Words*, was published by Spencer in 1999 to mark his 75th birthday.
5. Interview with Spencer, 28 March 1996.
6. A foretaste of this interest in graffiti can be seen in *Typographica*, OS no. 6, 1952, p. 3. Most of the page is occupied by a photograph (by the Australian designer Gordon Andrews) of a wall of St-Maximin Basilica, France covered by a dense web of graffiti scratches and marks,

similar in effect to an Abstract Expressionist 'field' painting. Similarly, the wrapper of *Typographica*, NS no. 2, December 1960 is taken from a photograph by Spencer of a tree trunk inscribed with letters, scratches and lovers' hearts, which is reproduced as a half-tone on the inside cover.

7. Spencer, H., 1967a, p. 4.

8. Jones, B., 'Chance', *Typographica*, NS no. 8, December 1963, pp. 21–2.

9. Spencer, H., 1967a, p. 3.

10. An exhibition of 29 of Spencer's photographs – taken in Italy, Crete, Ireland, France, Switzerland and Britain, from 1960 to 1972 – was shown at the Zelda Cheatle Gallery, 8 Cecil Court, London WC2, from 3 April to 3 May 1991. It included examples by John Berger, Bill Brandt, Henri Cartier-Bresson, Walker Evans, Fay Godwin, Ida Kar, William Klein, Eric de Maré, Roger Mayne, Lee Miller, Jean Mohr, Man Ray, Edwin Smith, Humphrey Spender, Josef Sudek and Edward Weston – all photographers admired by Spencer.

11. McClelland, R. D., 1973, p. 431.

12. Spencer commissioned de Maré to write about the 'lasting power' of black and white photography for *The Penrose Annual*. See de Maré, E., 1966. Spencer shares de Maré's preference: 'most serious photography is in black and white and I think it's because photography is taking things out of context and revealing the significance of something.' Interview with Spencer, 28 March 1996.

13. Eric de Maré, quoted in Woods, G. *et al.*, 1972, p. 100.

14. Interview with Spencer, 28 March 1996.

15. Middleton, M., 'Sunday photographers', *Typographica*, NS no. 9, June 1964, p. 42.

16. Interview with Spencer, 28 March 1996.

17. Editorial, *Typographica*, NS no. 4, December 1961, p. 1.

18. Spencer, H., 1961c, p. 3.

19. For an earlier, remarkably thorough example of photography of the environment used both as a taxonomical instrument and a campaigning weapon, see Nairn, I., 1955. Nairn's report, first published in June 1955, in *The Architectural Review*, documents the rapacious spread of 'Subtopia' by following, like Spencer, a predetermined route, in Nairn's case from Southampton to Gretna Green.

20. In 1961, Spencer, Reynolds Stone and Colin Forbes were asked by *Design* to respond to reports into experimental road signs, published by London Transport Executive and the Road Research Laboratory. See 'Lettering & legibility', *Design*, no. 152, August 1961, p. 61. For a more general discussion by Spencer of signposting issues, see Spencer, H., 1966b. Many of Spencer's photographs of street signs, including some unpublished anywhere else, were included in the visual survey *Signs in Action*. Sutton, J., 1965.

21. See *The Guardian*, 13 January 1962, *The Times Literary Supplement*, 6 April 1962, and Spencer, H., 1963e, pp. 24–9.

22. Agee, J. and Walker, E., 1960.

23. Interview with Spencer, 28 March 1996.

24. Letter to Spencer from John Berger, Geneva, 11 April 1963.

25. Letter to Spencer from John Berger, Geneva, 23 October 1963.

26. Mayne, R., 1961, unpaginated. See also Mayne, R., 1958, pp. 18–19 and 'Roger Mayne's Southam Street', reprinted with many of the photographs in Cheatle, Z., 1993, pp. 67–80.

27. Photographs by Euan Duff, Roger Mayne, Jane Gate and Peter Boyce were published in *Typographica*, NS no. 7, to accompany the exhibition 'Four photographers' at Lund Humphries, 12 Bedford Square, London WC1, from 16 to 30 May 1963.

28. Letter to Spencer from John Berger, Geneva, 23 October 1963.

29. Berger, J. and Mohr, J., 1989, p. 83. Berger

makes no direct reference to *Typographica* in the English edition. *Typographica* is, however, cited in a footnote in the French edition, *Une autre façon de raconter*, Paris: François Maspero, 1982, p. 83.

30. Letter to Spencer from John Berger, Geneva, 26 October 1964. Berger ends the letter: 'Did I tell you how much I admired your photographs of incongruity in Barbara Jones' article? [*Typographica*, NS no. 8] What a marvellous eye you have – for always the incongruity has a poetic (the poetry of human *wear*) resonance to it.'

31. Berger, J., 1965, p. 47.

32. Berger, J., 1965, p. 47.

33. Berger wrote again from Geneva on 2 January 1965, enclosing new versions of poems V and VI, as well as the awaited ninth poem and his article: 'Did you get my last letter suggesting a page of the photographs in sequence before printing them large and separately?' The description suggests he may not have been clear about Spencer's intention to present the poems and photographs as a separate booklet.

34. Dyer, G., 1986, p. 65.

35. For a reading of Berger and Mohr's collaboration, sensitive to the relationship between photograph and word, see Scott, C., 1999, pp. 252–91.

36. Berger, J., 1965, p. 45.

37. Berger, J., 1965, p. 47.

38. Berger, J. and Mohr, J., 1989, pp. 135–275.

5. Images and words are breeding

1. Hamilton, R., 'The books of Diter Rot', *Typographica*, NS no. 3, June 1961, p. 21.

2. Garland, K., 'Typophoto', *Typographica*, NS no. 3, June 1961, p. 19.

3. Hamilton, R., 'The books of Diter Rot', p. 21.

4. Spencer, H., 1961a, p. 53.

5. See *Fuse*, no. 10, 1994, 'Freeform' issue, featuring designs by Neville Brody, John Critchley, Tobias Frere Jones, Sylke Janesty, Cornel Windlin and Jon Wozencroft.

6. Fletcher, A., Forbes, C. and Gill, B., 1963, pp. 44, 66–7. Pages from *Bok 4a* (1961) and *Bok 1956–59* (1959) are shown.

7. Fletcher, A., Forbes, C. and Gill, B., 1963, pp. 66–7. Fletcher, Forbes and Gill have made Rot's work more 'graphic', and increased its contrast with the opposite page, by reversing it out of a black square.

8. Letter to Spencer from Franco Grignani, 15 May 1958. Spencer had evidently written to Grignani enclosing a copy of *Typographica*, OS no. 14, 1958. Finding the magazine 'more than interesting', Grignani writes of his intention 'to obtain all the back numbers'. Grignani went on to design the cover of *Typographica*, OS no. 16, 1959.

9. Extracts from *Watching words move* are also included in Fletcher, A., Forbes, C. and Gill, B., 1963, pp. 42–3. Somewhat misleadingly the authors – for graphic purposes – reassemble elements from many pages of BCG's notebook into the semblance of two much denser-packed pages.

10. Spencer, H., 1963c, p. 2.

11. Spencer, H., 1963c, p. 20.

12. The following designers are included in *17 Graphic Designers London*: Dennis Bailey, Derek Birdsall, George Daulby, George Mayhew, Peter Wildbur, Ian Bradbery, David Collins, Bob Gill, Alan Fletcher, Colin Forbes, Sydney King, Jock Kinneir, Margaret Calvert, Romek Marber, John Sewell, Barry Trengove, Tom Wolsey.

13. Blake, J. E., 1963, p. 45. See also Commander, J., 1963b, and Bigham, J., 1989.

14. See Blake, J. E., 1963, and Guyatt, R., 1963.

15. Adams, A., 1963.

16. Boxer, M., 'Ark', in Guyatt, R., 1963, p. 48.

For a detailed discussion of Pop Art-influenced graphic design in *Ark* magazine, see Seago, A., 1995, pp. 189–97.

17. Interview with Spencer, 17 August 1995.

18. Interview with Spencer, 7 March 1996.

19. Spencer delivered the paper 'Tradition: cliché, prison or basis of growth?' which was subsequently published in the *SIA Journal*. Spencer, H., 1958b.

20. Massey, A., 1995, p. 2.

21. See Robbins, D., 1990, pp. 137–49.

22. Banham, R., 1962/3.

23. Middleton, M., 'Sunday photographers', p. 35.

24. Spencer, H., 1987.

25. See Mahlow, D., 1963.

26. Gray, N., 'Art and writing: an exhibition', *Typographica*, NS no. 8, December 1963, p. 31.

27. Houédard, dom S., 'Concrete poetry & Ian Hamilton Finlay', *Typographica*, NS no. 8, December 1963, p. 49. An extract is reprinted in Bierut, M. *et al.*, 1999, pp. 146–9. For a critical assessment of Houédard's work and other writings by him, see Verey, C., 1972.

28. Letter to Spencer from Houédard, Prinknash Abbey, Gloucestershire, 24 August 1963. Further evidence that *Watching words move* was noticed by those interested in visual poetry, despite its origins within the professional design community, can be seen in the *Schrift und Bild* catalogue, in which extracts from the booklet are included. Mahlow. D., 1963, p. 174.

29. The first British exhibition of international concrete, phonetic and kinetic poetry was held at St Catherine's College, University of Cambridge, from 28 November to 5 December 1964. Finlay, Houédard and Stefan Themerson were among the exhibitors. *Typographica* was also shown. For surveys of concrete poetry, see Williams, E., 1967, and Wildman, E., 1970.

30. Reichardt, J., 1965a.

31. Reichardt, J., 1965b, p. 9.

32. Richard Hamilton supervised the printing

of the sheets of Rot's book at Lund Humphries' Bradford press, from specifications sent to him 'piecemeal' from Reykjavik, New York, Philadelphia, New Haven and Providence. The text of the 'review' that accompanies the sheet – in *Typographica*, NS no. 12, December 1965, p. 46 – is adapted from Hamilton's introductory text, published with the project. Hamilton describes the untitled artist's book as a new genre of 'graphic poetry'.

33. See Spencer, H., 1963a, and Themerson, S., 1965. Themerson used internal vertical justification in several works, including *Bayamus and the Theatre of Semantic Poetry* 1949, 1965), *Semantic Divertissements* (1946, 1962) and *St. Francis and the Wolf of Gubbio* (1972), all published by the Gaberbocchus Press. See Kubasiewicz, J. and Strauss, M., 1993. For a discussion of semantic composition and internal vertical justification, see Mayer, P., 1986.

34. Spencer, H., 1968, pp. 40–1.

35. 'Kurt Schwitters on a time-chart' was reprinted in The Netherlands by Huis Clos, in 1998, with a Dutch translation and an essay by Jasia Reichardt. Reichardt notes that the project, based on Themerson's lecture to the Society of Arts in Cambridge, had a nine-year gestation. The first version was sent to Spencer in March 1961. Themerson's final layout, with texts typed in black and red, stuck on illustrations and other collage elements, ran to 28 pages. After further adjustment, Spencer published a 20-page typeset version.

36. Spencer, H., 1967c, p. 3.

Exhibitions about *Typographica*

Herbert Spencer, Leeds
Institute Gallery, 1966

1965
21 April to 28 May
Gallery 303, 130 West 46th Street,
New York, USA (Organized by
The Composing Room)

3 July to 6 August
Walker Art Center, Minneapolis,
USA

29 September to 22 October
Monotype House, 43 Fetter Lane,
London, UK

1966
19 to 30 March
Leeds Institute Gallery, Cookridge
Street, Leeds, UK

Bibliography

Selected books and articles by Spencer

SPENCER, Herbert, 'Function & design in business printing', *Typographica*, OS no. 3, 1950, pp. 6–11.

——, *Design in Business Printing*, London: Sylvan Press, 1952a.

BELL, Anthony, MIDDLETON, Michael and SPENCER, Herbert, 'Introduction to the exhibition', *Typographica*, OS no. 5, 1952, pp. 3–4.

SPENCER, Herbert, 'Purpose and Pleasure', *Printing Review*, vol. 17 no. 60, winter 1952/3, pp. 21–4.

——, '"You are invited"', *Typographica*, OS no. 6, 1952b, pp. 21–3.

—— (ed.), *Designers in Britain*, vol. 4, London: Allan Wingate, 1954.

——, 'Recent developments in typography', *Ark*, no. 13, 1955a, pp. 20–3.

——, 'Stedelijk Museum catalogues', *Typographica*, OS no. 10, 1955b, pp. 5–11.

——, 'H. N. Werkman, printer-painter', *Typographica*, OS no. 11, 1955c, pp. 18–26.

—— (ed.), *Designers in Britain*, vol. 5, London: André Deutsch, 1957.

——, 'The publications of Gaberbocchus Press', *Typographica*, OS no. 14, 1958a, p. 4–11.

——, 'Tradition: cliché, prison or basis of growth?', *SIA Journal*, no. 66, July 1958b, p. 6, paper read by Spencer at 'The Art and Science of Typography', a conference organized by the New York Type Directors Club on 26 April 1958. Reprinted in Bierut, M. *et al.*, 1999.

——, 'The First International Conference on Typography, USA, 1958', *Graphis*, no. 80. vol. 14, November/December 1958c, pp. 546, 549.

——, 'Graphic design 4', *Design*, no. 132, December 1959, pp. 36–41.

——, 'Farewell to Trajan', *Typographica*, NS no. 1, June 1960 pp. 56–8.

——, 'The drawings of Alcopley', *Typographica*, NS no. 3, June 1961a, pp. 53–63.

——, 'No reason to be dull', *The Times Supplement on Design in Industry*, 4 October 1961b.

——, 'Mile-a-minute typography?', *Typographica*, NS no. 4, December 1961c, pp. 3–14.

——, 'Penguins on the march', *Typographica*, NS no. 5, June 1962, pp. 12–33.

——, *Printers and Designers*, London: Double Crown Club, 1963a.

——, 'The future of book production', *The Times Literary Supplement*, 26 April 1963b, p. 295.

——, 'Typography in Britain', *Typographica*, NS no. 7, May 1963c, pp. 2, 20.

——, 'Piet Zwart', *Typographica*, NS no. 7, May 1963d, pp. 25–32.

——, 'Which way where?', *The Silver Wheel*, inaugural number, 1963e, pp. 24–9.

——, 'The responsibilities of the design profession', *The Penrose Annual*, vol. 57, London: Lund Humphries, 1964, pp. 18–23. Reprinted in Bierut, M. *et al.*, 1999.

——, 'Typographica', *Idea*, vol. 12 no. 74, November 1965.

——, 'The designer and the printed word', *Vision 65*: International Center for the Typographic Arts, 1966a, paper read by Spencer at 'Vision 65', a conference sponsored by ICTA at Southern Illinois University on 21–23 October 1965.

——, 'Signposting', *RIBA Journal*, vol. 73 no. 12, December 1966b, pp. 550–9.

——, *Traces of Man*, London: Lund Humphries, 1967a.

——, 'The literate computer', *Queen*, 21 June 1967b, p. 70.

——, 'Typographica 1949–67', *Typographica*, NS no. 16, December 1967c, pp. 2–3.

——, *The Visible Word*, London: Royal College of Art, 1968.

——, *Pioneers of Modern Typography*, London: Lund Humphries, 1969, revised edn. 1982.

—— (ed.), *The Liberated Page*, London: Lund Humphries, 1987.

——, *Without Words*, London: self-published edn. of 250 copies, 1999.

140

Selected articles on Spencer and *Typographica*

ADAMS, Anthony, review of *Typographica*, NS no. 7, *Design*, no. 179, November 1963, p. 77.

'Contemporary typography and graphic art', review of *Typographica*, OS no. 1, British Federation of Master Printers' *Members Circular*, vol. 48 no. 9, September 1949.

DAVIS, Alec, 'House style for a printer', *Design*, no. 108, December 1957, pp. 44–6.

——, 'House style by remote control', *Design*, no. 118, October 1958, pp. 45–7.

FACETTI, Germano, review of *Typographica*, NS no. 3, *Design*, no. 155, November 1961, pp. 77, 79.

FARRELLY, Liz, 'Traces of man', *Eye*, no. 3 vol. 1, spring 1991, pp. 64–9.

FLETCHER, Alan, 'Herbert Spencer', *Typos*, no. 2, 1981, pp. 18–20.

FORBES, Colin, review of *Typographica*, NS no. 1, *Design*, no. 142, October 1960, pp. 93, 95.

FROSHAUG, Anthony, 'Typography ancient and modern', *Studio International*, vol. 180 no. 924, July/August 1970, pp. 60–1.

GILL, Bob, review of *Typographica*, NS no. 2, *Design*, no. 148, April 1961, p. 95.

HATCH, Peter, 'Businesslike printing', *Design*, no. 41, May 1952, p. 34.

——, review of *Typographica*, OS no. 14, *Design*, no. 118, October 1958, p. 71.

HAZZLEWOOD, John W., 'Printer's profile 4: Herbert Spencer', *The Cornerstone*, no. 4 vol. 1, September 1954, pp. 52–4.

'Herbert Spencer', *Printing Review*, vol. 18 no. 64, winter 1953–4, pp. 28–30.

HICKSON, Stanley, 'Book production feature no. 63', review of *Typographica*, NS no. 4, *British Books*, April 1962.

——, review of *Typographica*, NS no. 7, *British Books*, August 1963.

——, 'Book production feature no. 69', review of *Typographica*, NS no. 8, *British Books*, March 1964.

——, review of *Typographica*, NS no. 11, *British Books*, September 1965.

——, 'Book production feature no. 76', review of *Typographica*, NS no. 12, *British Books*, April 1966.

——, review of *Typographica*, NS no. 15, *The Publisher*, October/November 1967.

HIGGINS, Dick, review of *The Liberated Page*, *Small Press*, February 1988, p. 30.

KINROSS, Robin, review of *Pioneers of Modern Typography*, *Design Issues*, vol. 1 no. 1, spring 1984, pp. 89–91.

——, review of *The Liberated Page*, *Blueprint*, no. 42, November 1987, p. 56.

——, 'Herbert Spencer', in Colin Naylor (ed.), *Contemporary Designers*, 2nd edn., Chicago and London: St James Press, 1990, pp. 527–8.

——, 'Eclectic seduction' (letter), *Eye*, no. 32 vol. 8, summer 1999, p. 4.

McCLELLAND, Robert D., 'Expressive patterns: the work of Herbert Spencer', *The British Journal of Photography*, vol. 120 no. 5,886, 11 May 1973, pp. 428–31.

MAIN, James, review of *Typographica*, NS no. 5, *Design*, no. 168, December 1962, p. 87.

'Men of Letters', *The Times Literary Supplement*, 6 April 1962.

MEYER, J. J., 'Herbert Spencer: ein englischer Typograph', *Gebrauchsgraphik*, vol. 31, November 1960, pp. 42–7.

MOORE, Gordon, review of *Typographica*, no. 12, *Ark*, no. 18, November 1956, p. 69.

'Notable typographers: no. 1 – Herbert Spencer', *The Griffith Graph*, August 1957, p. 2.

OVERTON, Frank, review of *Typographica*, NS no. 6, *Design*, no. 173, May 1963, p. 66.

PLATA, Walter, 'Herbert Spencer', *Typographische Monatsblätter*, no. 11, November 1958, pp. 577–84.

——, 'Moderne Englische typografie: Herbert Spencer', *Der Druckspiegel*, 1959.

POYNOR, Rick, *Modernism and Eclecticism: Typographica, 1949–67*, unpublished MPhil thesis, London: Royal College of Art, 1998.

——, '*Typographica*: modernism and eclecticism', *Eye*, no. 31 vol. 8, spring 1999, pp. 64–75.

Review of *Typographica*, NS no. 12, *British Printer*, February 1966.

SEWELL, John, review of *Typographica*, OS no. 9, *Ark*, no. 12, autumn 1954, p. 55.

SMITH, Bryan H., 'Penrose portrait: Herbert Spencer', *The Penrose Annual*, vol. 68, London: Lund Humphries, 1975, pp. 193–208.

SPENCER, Herbert, 'Getting going: Herbert Spencer', *Designer*, January 1980, pp. 6–8.

STIFF, Paul, 'Design for reading', *Graphics World*, no. 75, November/December 1988, pp. 31, 33.

TRACY, Walter, review of *Typographica*, OS no. 2, *Design*, no. 17, May 1950, p. 22.

——, review of *Typographica*, OS no. 6, *Design*, no. 49, January 1953, p. 34.

'The value of asymmetry', review of *Typographica*, OS no. 3, *The British & Colonial Printer*, 16 March 1951.

VICKERS, Graham, 'True to type', *Design Week*, vol. 2 no. 39, 2 October 1987, p. 21.

141

General books and articles

AGEE, James and EVANS, Walker, *Let Us Now Praise Famous Men*, Boston: Houghton Mifflin, 1960, first published in 1941.

ALPHABET AND IMAGE, 1946–8.

APOLLONIO, Umbro, *Futurist Manifestos*, London: Thames and Hudson, 1973.

ARK, 1950–64.

BANHAM, Mary and HILLIER, Bevis (eds.), *A Tonic to the Nation: The Festival of Britain 1951*, London: Thames and Hudson, 1976.

BANHAM, Reyner, 'Who is this "Pop"?', *Motif*, no. 10, winter 1962/3, pp. 3–13.

BAYER, Herbert, GROPIUS, Walter and GROPIUS, Ise, *Bauhaus 1919–1928*, London: Secker and Warburg, 1975, first published by the Museum of Modern Art, New York, 1938.

BERGER, John and MOHR, Jean, *A Fortunate Man: The Story of a Country Doctor*, London: Allen Lane, The Penguin Press, 1967.

——and——, *Another Way of Telling*, Cambridge: Granta Books, 1989.

BIERUT, Michael, HELFAND, Jessica, HELLER, Steven and POYNOR, Rick, *Looking Closer 3: Classic Writings on Graphic Design*, New York: Allworth Press, 1999.

BIGHAM, Julia, *The Designers and Art Directors Association in the 1960s: A Reflection of Changes in Graphic Design and Advertising*, unpublished MA thesis, London: Royal College of Art, 1989.

BLAKE, John E., 'Communication and persuasion', *Design*, no. 140, August 1960, pp. 32–5.

——, 'Two exhibitions with a common message', *Design*, no. 175, July 1963, pp. 37–45.

——, 'Growing pains of a new profession', *Design*, no. 197, May 1965, pp. 28–35.

BLAUVELT, Andrew, 'Foreword: Disciplinary bodies: the resistance to theory and the cut of the critic', in Andrew Blauvelt (ed.), *Visible Language*, 'New Perspectives: Critical Histories of Graphic Design', vol. 28 no. 3, spring 1994.

BOWLER, Berjouhi, *The Word as Image*, London: Studio Vista, 1970.

BOWMAN, John, *Crete*, London: Secker and Warburg, 1962.

BROOS, Kees and HEFTING, Paul, *Dutch Graphic Design*, London: Phaidon Press, 1993.

BUCHER, Annemarie, *Spirale: Eine Künstlerzeitschrift 1953–1964*, Baden: Verlag Lars Müller, 1990.

CAPLAN, David (ed.), *Designers in Britain*, vol. 6, London: André Deutsch, 1964.

CHEATLE, Zelda *et al.*, *The Street Photographs of Roger Mayne*, London: Zelda Cheatle Press, 1993.

COMMANDER, John, *17 Graphic Designers London*, London: Balding and Mansell, 1963a.

——, 'Design & Art Direction '63', *Graphis*, no. 109 vol. 19, 1963b, pp. 363–75.

DESIGN, 1949–68.

DRUCKER, Johanna, *The Visible Word: Experimental Typography and Modern Art, 1909–1923*, Chicago and London: University of Chicago Press, 1994.

DUCHAMP, Marcel, *The Bride stripped bare by her bachelors, even*, London: Lund Humphries and New York: George Wittenborn, 1960.

DYER, Geoff, *Ways of Telling: The Work of John Berger*, London: Pluto Press, 1986.

FLEISCHMANN, Gerd, BOSSHARD, Hans Rudolf and BIGNENS, Christoph, *Max Bill: Typografie, Reklame, Buchgestaltung*, Zurich: Niggli, 1999.

FLEMING, Allan, 'The tired typographer', *Design*, no. 146, February 1961a, p. 65.

——, 'As others see us – a Canadian designer looks at British typography', *Print in Britain*, April 1961b, pp. 380–81.

FLETCHER, Alan, 'Letter from America', *Ark*, no. 19, 1957, pp. 36–9.

FLETCHER, Alan, FORBES, Colin and GILL, Bob, *Graphic Design: Visual Comparisons*, London: Studio Books, 1963.

GARLAND, Ken, 'Graphic design 5: illustrated periodicals', *Design*, no. 135, March 1960a, pp. 31–7.

——, 'Structure and substance', in Allan Delafons (ed.), *The Penrose Annual*, vol. 54, London: Lund Humphries, 1960b, pp. 1–10.

——, 'A long, long trail a-winding', 1988, in *A Word in Your Eye: Opinions, Observations and Conjectures on Design, from 1960 to the present*, Reading: University of Reading, 1996.

——, 'Graphic design in Britain 1951–61: a personal memoir', in *A Word in Your Eye*, 1996.

GERSTNER, Karl and KUTTER, Markus, *Die neue Grafik*, Teufen: Niggli, 1959.

GRAY, Camilla, *The Great Experiment: Russian Art 1863–1922*, London: Thames and Hudson, 1962.

GRAY, Nicolette (Nicolete), *Nineteenth Century Ornamented Types and Title Pages*, London: Faber and Faber, 1938, new edn. 1976.

GUYATT, Richard *et al.*, *Graphics RCA: Fifteen years' work of the School of Graphic Design, Royal College of Art*, London: Lion and Unicorn Press, 1963.

HALIDAY, Nigel Vaux, *More than a Bookshop: Zwemmer's and Art in the 20th Century*, London: Philip Wilson Publishers, 1991.

HAMILTON, Richard, 'Towards a typographical rendering of The Green Box', *Uppercase*, no. 2, 1959, unpaginated.

——, *Collected Words*, London: Thames and Hudson, 1982.

HARLING, Robert, 'Victorian revival', in R. B. Fishenden (ed.), *The Penrose Annual*, vol. 41, 1939, pp. 73–6.

——, 'Fingermarks and decoration', *Image*, no. 2, autumn 1949, pp. 1–2.

142

HARRISON, Martin, *Young Meteors: British Photojournalism: 1957–1965*, London: Jonathan Cape, 1998.

HASLER, Charles, *A Specimen of Display Letters Designed for the Festival of Britain 1951*, London: Typography Panel of the Festival of Britain, 1951.

HIGGOTT, Andrew, 'Eric de Maré and the functional tradition', in *Eric de Maré: Photographer Builder with Light*, London: Architectural Association, 1990.

HOLLIS, Richard, *Graphic Design: A Concise History*, London: Thames and Hudson, 1994.

HOMANS, Katy, *Robert Brownjohn: conceptual design*, unpublished MFA thesis, New Haven: Yale University, 1982.

——, 'BJ', *Eye*, no. 4 vol. 1, 1991, pp. 52–63.

HOWE, Ellic, *A visit to Lund Humphries*, London: Lund Humphries, undated (1950s).

HUGHES, Quentin J., 'Expressive pattern', *RIBA Journal*, May 1968.

HURLBURT, Allen, *Publication Design: A Guide to Page Layout, Typography, Format and Style*, New York: Van Nostrand Reinhold, 1971.

JEFFREY, Ian, *Photography: A Concise History*, London: Thames and Hudson, 1981.

JONES, Barbara, *The Unsophisticated Arts*, London: The Architectural Press, 1951.

KINROSS, Robin, 'New typography in Britain after 1945', in Nicola Hamilton (ed.), *From the Spitfire to the Microchip: Studies in the History of Design from 1945*, London: The Design Council, 1985, pp. 45–53.

——, *Modern Typography: An Essay in Critical History*, London: Hyphen Press, 1992.

——, *Anthony Froshaug: Typography & Texts* and *Anthony Froshaug: Documents of a Life* (2 vols.), London: Hyphen Press, 2000.

KOSTELANETZ, Richard (ed.), *Moholy-Nagy: An Anthology*, New York: Da Capo Press, 1970.

——, *Dictionary of the Avant-Gardes*, Pennington, NJ: A Cappella Books, 1993.

KUBASIEWICZ, Jan and STRAUSS, Monica, *The Themersons and the Gaberbocchus Press – An Experiment in Publishing, 1949–1979*, New York: MJS Books & Graphics, 1993.

'Lettering & legibility', *Design*, no. 152, August 1961, pp. 56–61.

LEWIS, John and BRINKLEY, John, *Graphic Design with Special Reference to Lettering, Typography and Illustration*, London: Routledge and Kegan Paul, 1954.

LEWIS, John, *Typography: Basic Principles: Influences and Trends since the 19th Century*, London: Studio Books, 1963.

——, *Printed Ephemera: The Changing Use of Type and Letterforms in English and American Printing*, London: Faber and Faber, 1969, first published by W. S. Cowell in 1962.

MacCARTHY, Fiona, *British Design since 1880: A Visual History*, London: Lund Humphries, 1982.

McLEAN, Ruari, *Magazine Design*, London: Oxford University Press, 1969.

——, *Jan Tschichold: Typographer*, London: Lund Humphries, 1975.

——, *The Thames and Hudson Manual of Typography*, London: Thames and Hudson, 1980, revised edn. 1992.

—— (ed.), *Typographers on Type*, London: Lund Humphries, 1995.

MAHLOW, Dietrich, *Schrift und Bild*, Amsterdam: Stedelijk Museum, 1963.

DE MARÉ, Eric, 'The lasting power of black-and-white', in Herbert Spencer (ed.), *The Penrose Annual*, vol. 59, 1966, pp. 28–42.

MASSEY, Anne, *The Independent Group: Modernism and Mass Culture in Britain, 1945–59*, Manchester: Manchester University Press, 1995.

MASSIN, (Robert), *Letter and Image*, London: Studio Vista, 1970.

MAYER, Hansjörg, ROT, Dieter (Diter) and SOHM, H. (eds.), *Dieter Rot Collected Works Volume 20: Books and Graphics (part 1) from 1947 until 1971*, Stuttgart, London and Reykjavik: Edition Hansjörg Mayer, 1972.

MAYER, Peter, 'Semantic composition', *Octavo*, no. 2, 1986, pp. 2–5.

——, 'Concrete poems just *are*', *Eye*, no. 20 vol. 5, spring 1996, pp. 70–7.

MAYNE, Roger, 'Photographs', *Ark*, no. 23, autumn 1958, pp. 18–19.

——, 'Portrait of Southam Street by Roger Mayne', *Uppercase*, no. 5, 1961, unpaginated.

MEGGS, Philip B., *A History of Graphic Design*, 2nd edn., New York: Van Nostrand Reinhold, 1992.

MELLOR, David, *The Sixties Art Scene in London*, London: Phaidon Press, 1993.

—— et al., *Fifty Years of the Future: A chronicle of the Institute of Contemporary Arts 1947–1997*, London: Institute of Contemporary Arts, 1998.

MERMOZ, Gérard, 'Masks on hire: in search of typographic histories', in Andrew Blauvelt (ed.), *Visible Language*, 'New Perspectives: Critical Histories of Graphic Design', vol. 28 no. 3, spring 1994, pp. 261–85.

MIDDLETON, Michael, *Soldiers of Lead*, London: The Labour Party, 1948.

MOORE, Barbara and HENDRICKS, Jon, 'The page as alternative space 1950–1969', in Joan Lyons (ed.), *Artists' Books: A Critical Anthology and Source Book*, New York: Visual Studies Workshop Press, 1985, pp. 87–95.

MORA, Gilles and HILL, John T., *Walker Evans: The Hungry Eye*, London: Thames and Hudson, 1993.

MOTIF, 1958–67.

MÜLLER-BROCKMANN, Josef, *The Graphic Artist and his Design Problems*, Teufen: Niggli, 1961.

MYERSON, Jeremy, *Beware Wet Paint: Designs by Alan Fletcher*, London: Phaidon, 1996.

NAIRN, Ian, *Outrage*, London: The Architectural Press, 1955.

143